D0542655

VEGETARIAN COOKING

THROUGH THE YEAR

VEGETARIAN COOKING

THROUGH THE YEAR

Sarah Bounds

CHANCELLOR
PRESS

Note

1 All recipes serve four unless otherwise stated.
2 All spoon measurements are level.
3 All eggs are sizes 3, 4 unless otherwise stated. Although free-range eggs are specified throughout, you can use ordinary eggs when the former are unobtainable.
4 Preparation times given are an average calculated during recipe testing.
5 Metric and Imperial measurements have been calculated separately. Use one set of measurements only as they are not exact equivalents.
6 Cooking times may vary slightly depending on the individual oven. Dishes should be placed in the centre of the oven unless otherwise specified.
7 Always preheat the oven or grill to the specified temperature.
8 Although these recipes do not contain salt, you can add a little to taste, if preferred.

First published in 1986 by Argus Health Publications
under the title *Creative Vegetarian*
Revised edition published in 1987 by
The Hamlyn Publishing Group Limited
under the title *Seasonal Vegetarian*

This 1993 edition published by
Chancellor Press
an imprint of Reed Consumer Books Limited
Michelin House, 81 Fulham Road, London SW3 6RB
and Auckland, Melbourne, Singapore and Toronto

Copyright © Argus Health Publications Limited 1986 and 1987

Photography by David Jordan
Photographic styling by Pip Kelly

All rights reserved. No part of this publication may be
reproduced, stored in a retrieval system, or transmitted
in any form or by any means, electronic, mechanical,
photocopying, recording or otherwise, without the prior
permission of the copyright holder.

ISBN 1 85152 267 0

A CIP catalogue record for this book is available
at the British Library

Printed in Malaysia

CONTENTS

INTRODUCTION

Healthy eating from January to December is the aim of this book. With the emphasis firmly on vegetarian meals to suit the season, I hope that there is something for everyone to enjoy, including those not committed to vegetarian eating. As the recipes in each of the four sections show, a vegetarian diet is fun and full of variety whether it be the depths of winter or the height of summer.

Planning a Healthy Diet without Meat

Most people's first thoughts on becoming vegetarian, or simply on cutting down the amount of meat, fish and poultry in their diets are concerned with health. Is it possible to stay healthy without meat? Where do vitamins and minerals come from and what about protein? What can I eat instead of just cheese, eggs and milk? The answers to these questions are positive; cutting meat, fish and poultry from your diet does not mean that you will go short of vital nutrients like protein, vitamins and minerals. In fact, research suggests that a vegetarian diet is positively healthier than a non-vegetarian diet and that common problems like obesity are less likely to occur for vegetarians than their meat-eating neighbours.

Protein Power

We all associate animal foods like meat, fish, eggs, cheese and milk with protein and it is true that these foods do all supply good levels of high-quality protein. Taken individually, foods of vegetable origin tend to be less concentrated sources of protein and the protein they do contain is of a lower quality.

However, provided a mixture of different kinds of vegetable food is eaten, the protein is of equally good quality to that in animal foods. The quality of protein in a food is assessed in terms of the amounts of the eight essential amino acids necessary for health, found in that food. Animal protein-containing foods contain all the essential amino acids and in amounts suitable to meet the body's needs; plant protein-containing foods on the other hand may lack one or more of the essential amino acids or contain an insufficient quantity.

Plant protein-containing foods fall into two main groups and each group is short of a different amino acid. To obtain the balance of the amino acids essential for the body at one time it is important to mix different plant foods together at one meal. So a pulse should be eaten with a grain or nut or seed and so on, as the chart below shows. Alternatively the shortage of amino acids in, say, rice, can be overcome by adding a dairy food—milk, egg or cheese—at the same meal.

Remembering the basic rule of combining plant protein foods will ensure that a vegetarian diet remains a healthy alternative to a diet which includes, or is based on, meat.

Combining plant foods for protein

To make the most of the protein found in plant foods, combine pulses and grains or nuts or seeds at as many meals as possible.

Pulses

Beans: butter, haricot, aduki, blackeye, flageolet, red and black kidney beans, pinto and soya beans.

Lentils: red, green and continental brown lentils.

Peas: green and yellow dried split peas.

Grains, Nuts and Seeds

Grains: oats, wheat, barley, rye, millet, buckwheat, corn or maize, rice. These should be eaten preferably in the whole-grain state, or as flour milled from the whole grain.

Nuts: walnuts, hazelnuts, cashews, almonds, brazils, pecans, peanuts and chestnuts.

Seeds: sesame, sunflower and pumpkin.

Fibre

Although individually animal foods may have a superior protein content to that of vegetable foods, they do not contain fibre. It is from plant foods that the dietary fibre so vital in a healthy diet, comes. Foods such as the protein-rich pulses, grains, nuts and seeds all supply fibre, as do fruits and vegetables. Ideally, foods should be eaten as little processed as possible to maximise fibre content — wholegrain cereals such as brown rice contain more fibre than their refined counterparts. Eating a vegetarian diet, with the emphasis on plant rather than animal foods, makes it far easier to include the 30 g recommended daily intake of fibre.

Fat

Foods high in fat are concentrated sources of calories and are undesirable in a healthy diet. There is now universal agreement among doctors and nutritionists that the typical British diet contains far too much fat, and in particular that the amount of saturated fat should be reduced. We need to restrict fat intake to 115 g a day. Saturated fats tend to be found in animal foods such as meat, offal and dairy produce. Fish, poultry and plant foods are generally higher in polyunsaturated fatty acids which are desirable ingredients in the diet.

Eating a vegetarian diet tends to reduce the level of saturated fat in favour of polyunsaturated fat and this is seen as beneficial. However, avoid adding extra fat to food, which will undo some of the good achieved by eliminating meat from the diet. First, it is important to try to limit the amount of extra fat used in cooking — grilling, steaming and baking avoid the addition of extra fat, whereas roasting and frying usually involve adding quite large amounts of extra fat to food. Secondly, it is important not to swamp food in fat at the table — adding a knob of butter to cooked vegetables obviously boosts not just the amount of fat but the calories too. Thirdly, it's wise to watch out for highly processed foods which may contain much added fat that's 'hidden' — cakes, pastries and biscuits usually depend on a high level of fat for their flavour and texture. It is not essential to avoid these items totally but they should be restricted to treats.

The recipes in this book aim to help restrict the amount of fat being eaten and because they are vegetarian, they tend to contain the beneficial polyunsaturated fatty acids rather than the harmful saturated fats.

Vitamins and Minerals

Eating a meat-free diet does not mean that the body is deprived of essential vitamins and minerals, any more than it is of protein or other important nutrients. Eating a wide range of different foods is the key to a healthy diet. This list should help you check that vital vitamins and minerals are present in your diet. The foods listed under each vitamin and mineral contain the vitamin or mineral in decreasing order of quantity, so the best sources are listed first. Try to ensure that each day your diet contains a good source of every nutrient.

Vitamins

A: (plant foods contain carotene which the body converts to retinol, vitamin A). Carrots, parsley, spinach, turnip tops, spring greens, sweet potatoes, watercress, broccoli, melon, endives, pumpkin, apricots, lettuce, prunes, tomatoes, peaches, butter, margarine, cheese and eggs.

B1 (thiamine): brewer's yeast, yeast extract, brown rice, wheatgerm, nuts, soya flour, oats and wholemeal bread.

B2 (riboflavin): yeast extract, brewer's yeast, wheatgerm, cheese, eggs, wheatbran, soya flour, yogurt, milk, leafy green vegetables, pulses.

B3 (niacin): yeast extract, brewer's yeast, wheatbran, nuts, soya flour, wheat, cheese, dried fruit, wholemeal bread, brown rice, wheatgerm, oats, eggs, pulses.

B6 (pyridoxine): brewer's yeast, wheatbran, yeast extract, wheatgerm, oats, soya flour, bananas, whole wheat, nuts, brown rice, potatoes, leafy green vegetables, root vegetables, wholemeal bread and eggs.

Pantothenic acid: brewer's yeast, yeast extract, nuts, bran, wheatgerm, soya flour, eggs, oats, pulses, dried fruits, maize, rice and wholemeal bread.

Biotin: brewer's yeast, yeast extract, eggs, oats, wheatbran, wheatgerm, wholemeal bread, maize.

Folic acid: brewer's yeast, soya flour,

wheatgerm, wheatbran, nuts, leafy green vegetables, pulses, oats, whole wheat, wholemeal bread, citrus fruits, bananas, cheese.

B12 (cobalamin): eggs, cheese, milk. Plant foods do not contain B12 so vegans need to take special care in obtaining this vitamin. Some fermented plant foods such as soya-based miso, do contain some B12, and manufacturers of yeast extract products sometimes add it to their product.

C: blackcurrants, guavas, parsley, kale, horseradish, broccoli tops, green peppers, tomato purée, Brussels sprouts, chives, lemons, cauliflower, watercress, strawberries, cabbage, oranges, mustard and cress, blackberries, gooseberries, grapefruit, lychees. Other fruit and vegetables contain less than 40 mg vitamin C in 100 g/4 oz.

D: eggs, goat's milk, cow's milk, butter and margarine, cheese. Vitamin D is also made in the body by the action of sunlight.

E: vegetable oils, nuts, muesli, eggs, brown rice, peas and beans.

Minerals

There are many minerals known to be essential for health, some required in quite large amounts, others in comparatively small quantities. Some of these vital minerals are present in a wide range of foods and a shortage is unlikely to occur. Phosphorus, sodium and chlorine are three examples of abundant minerals. Sodium in particular is eaten in far greater quantities in Britain than is needed for health and there is some evidence to suggest that the excessive amounts of sodium often eaten are hazardous and perhaps likely to aggravate the problem of high blood pressure. Limiting the amount of sodium eaten as salt is not difficult and will not have harmful consequences (except for kidney patients whose diets need to be supervised in this respect). For this reason salt has been omitted from the recipes in this book, as it is widely added to processed foods such as cheese, bread, breakfast cereals and sodium itself is naturally present in many fresh fruits and vegetables.

These minerals apart, there are a number of minerals which the body needs in quite large quantities and these are listed here together with the foods containing the best quantities of each. Zinc is one mineral of particular significance to vegetarians and vegans because the zinc in plant foods is less well absorbed than that from animal foods, so it is important to eat zinc-rich food daily to ensure supply is adequate.

Calcium: hard cheeses, soft cheeses, nuts, pulses, milk, root vegetables, eggs, oatmeal, fruits, wholemeal flour, maize.
Iron: brewer's yeast, wheatbran, cocoa, soya flour, parsley, dried peaches, figs and apricots, oatmeal, spinach, wholemeal flour, prunes, wholemeal bread, beans, sultanas and raisins.
Magnesium: soya beans, nuts, brewer's yeast, wholemeal flour, brown rice, dried peas, wholemeal bread, rye, bananas, dried fruits and fresh vegetables.
Potassium: dried fruits, soya flour, molasses, wheatbran, raw salad vegetables, nuts, muesli, fresh fruit, cooked vegetables, wholemeal bread and flour, eggs, cheese and brown rice.
Zinc: brewer's yeast, cheese, wholemeal bread, eggs, carrots, peanuts, rice, tomatoes, peas, sweetcorn.

Microwave cooking

Many people associate microwave cooking with convenience. A microwave oven is without doubt a time-saving appliance and it is useful for reheating convenience foods or ready-prepared dishes. It can also be used to cook fresh, healthy ingredients with great success, saving on time and effort.

How do microwaves cook food

Microwave ovens cook food by friction. The microwaves generated within the oven are absorbed by food, causing the minute particles within the food to vibrate rapidly. As they do so they generate heat by friction. The microwave energy penetrates approximately 2.5–5 cm/1–2 in into the food and the heat produced by this friction is passed to other areas of the food by conduction. So those areas of thick or deep food where the microwaves themselves cannot penetrate are cooked by the conduction of the heat.

Microwaves are transmitted through some materials such as glass (Pyrex), glazed pottery or ceramics and paper, so while the food absorbs microwaves, the cooking utensils do not. Metallic dishes or materials glazed with a metal, reflect the microwaves and cause them to bounce back to the walls of the oven without reaching the food.

What will cook
Some foods are ideally suited to microwave cooking, others less so and some just cannot be cooked in the microwave at all. Ideally use the microwave oven to cook foods where there is a positive benefit – either by saving time, by reducing the number of utensils used to prepare a dish or by improving the quality of the finished dish. There are some foods, such as brown rice, wholemeal pasta and the larger pulses (beans or chickpeas), which do not cook quicker in the microwave oven, so cook these conventionally. Other foods, like fresh fruit and vegetables, dried fruits (such as prunes and apricots), baked potatoes and airy foods (such as scrambled egg) all cook quickly and well in the microwave oven. Sauces, both roux based and tomato based are also easily prepared in the microwave.

Convenience really is the key word to microwave cooking but remember that food does cook quickly so it is vital always to set the cooking time precisely. Food overcooked in a microwave is not only disasterous but it can also be potentially dangerous.

Advantages of microwave cooking
1 Lighter, easier to handle dishes can be used in place of heavy or cumbersome saucepans and often fewer utensils are required, saving on washing up.
2 Cooking and reheating times are quicker, requiring smaller amounts of fluid and resulting in better retention of vitamins B and C, and vital minerals which are otherwise dissolved in cooking liquids.
3 Sauces, soups, stews and other recipes that benefit from being made in advance and left overnight for flavours to develop, can be reheated simply and efficiently in the microwave oven.
4 Microwaves thaw out frozen food quickly and evenly – useful if you need to use food from the freezer when there is insufficient time to defrost it at room temperature.

Simple rules to ensure success
1 Cover food during cooking to speed up the process by retaining moisture. Ideally use a covered ovenproof glass casserole dish (for example, Pyrex). Alternatively cover with a microwave cling film that is free from plasticisers (and will be labelled as such). Remember to pierce the film to allow steam to escape. If it is too tightly sealed and air cannot escape, then steam will build up within the dish and the cling film may burst. For the same reason, always unseal bags or boxes and pierce egg yolks, potatoes, tomatoes or apples for baking whole to allow air to escape.
2 Some microwave ovens incorporate a stirrer – a rotating device located in the roof of the oven – to distribute the waves within the oven cavity. The majority of ovens also have turntables. Check to make sure that the food is cooking evenly and turn it round or stir it if necessary.
3 The food on the outside of the dish cooks quicker than that in the centre, so arrange foods such as cauliflower florets or broccoli spears with the thicker stems to the outside.
4 Always follow the manufacturer's instructions. Before following recipes always check to see which power oven was used for testing. The microwave notes in this book were prepared for an oven with an output of 650 watts. If the power output of your oven is lower than this, allow slightly longer cooking times; if higher, then reduce the times slightly. For example if your microwave oven has an output of 700 watts, then the cooking times will be slightly quicker than those suggested in the notes.

Freezing
As well as the obvious use of the freezer for storing surplus seasonal fresh fruits and vegetables, the freezer makes a perfect partner to the microwave oven in which ready-made meals prepared with fresh seasonal produce can be thawed out quickly.

GLOSSARY

HERBS AND SPICES

Natural herbs and spices are important ingredients in healthy cooking, adding a depth of flavour and interest to foods which helps to replace or eliminate salt in the diet. A high intake of salt has been linked to high blood pressure which can increase the chances of developing heart disease or having a stroke. It has also been linked to the unpleasant problems of fluid retention.

None of the recipes in this book contain salt (with the exception of the recipe for home-made bread, where a little salt is essential). The recipes here have sufficient flavour from the natural foods themselves or from the use of herbs and spices. These natural flavourings really are an essential item in the store cupboard of the vegetarian cook, helping to give plant foods like grains and beans an extra depth of flavour that makes them really quite delicious to eat. The following list is by no means an essential list, it is simply a guide to readily available herbs and spices, which can be used in healthy cooking.

HERBS

Basil: an excellent accompaniment to tomatoes in salads, or cooked in sauces, soups, pizzas and other Mediterranean dishes.

Bay Leaves: a good all-round herb suitable for flavouring casseroles, sauces and soups. Always remember to discard before serving or before liquidising mixtures.

Bouquet Garni: a bunch of herbs added to soups, sauces or casseroles. It usually consists of a bay leaf, thyme and parsley tied neatly. The herbs can be varied to suit the recipe – rosemary, marjoram, chives, basil or mint can be added. Discard the bouquet garni before serving the dish.

Chervil: a good herb to use with carrots, or in carrot soup, as well as generally with salads or with egg-based recipes.

Chives: these are at their best simply chopped and scattered over salads or used to garnish cooked dishes – such as baked potatoes, soups and sauces.

Coriander Leaves: fresh coriander leaves are similar in appearance to flat-leafed parsley. They have a distinct aroma and flavour. Chopped, the leaves are used as a flavouring for a variety of dishes or they can be used as a garnish.

Dill: the fresh leaves or the seeds of this herb can be used to complement vegetables such as cabbage, cucumber, courgettes and celery. It is also useful to flavour vinegar and salad dressings.

Fennel: the fine feathery leaves of fennel can be chopped and mixed with other herbs to give full 'mixed' herb flavour or they can be used to enhance the flavour of salad dressings.

Garlic: look out for plump, fresh heads of garlic. If you use a lot of garlic, then buy a string which can be hung in a cool dry place to provide enough for several months. The peeled cloves can be chopped or crushed before use in a broad variety of hot or cold recipes.

Horseradish: best known as the sauce, the root can also be used to liven up dressings for root vegetable salads and goes particularly well with beetroot.

Lemon Balm: adds a delicate flavour to fruit dishes and also makes a refreshing herb tea.

Marjoram: used in Mediterranean food with olive oil and vegetables like tomatoes, courgettes and aubergines. It is also good in nut roasts, burgers and stuffings to give a full flavour.

Mint: good in teas, but also ideal for chilled soups or yogurt-based salad dressings. It is also good for complementing potatoes and cucumbers. Also essential for bringing out the flavour of new potatoes.

Oregano: another herb which lends itself to Mediterranean cuisine with tomato-based dishes. Also good with savoury nut dishes, in vegetable omelettes or with pulses.

Parsley: so often used simply as a garnish, freshly chopped parsley is also excellent in giving flavour to savoury stuffings, nut roasts and burgers.

Rosemary: complements leeks and onions well and is good in quiches, omelettes and with other herbs to give a full flavour.

Sage: ideal for rich nut mixtures and in flavouring beans and cheese dishes.

Savoury: either winter savoury or summer savoury according to their seasonal availability. A strongly flavoured herb that lends itself to most savoury cooking in the same way as thyme.

Sorrel: the leaves of sorrel make a good addition to green salads and can even be lightly cooked to replace spinach, if there is an abundant supply.

Tarragon: a distinctive flavour which goes well with courgettes, leeks, mushrooms and tomatoes. Also good with egg and other dairy products.

Thyme: widely used in all types of savoury dishes. Excellent all-round herb, but especially good with mushrooms.

SPICES

Cardamom: whole pods, either black or green which add distinctive flavour. Ground cardamom is also available; usually used in combination with other Indian spices.

Cayenne: powdered hot chillies, cayenne adds colour and hot flavour to food and can be used as a garnish too.

Chillies: fresh chillies are best, and used in Chilli Beans, and in many Indian dishes. Dried red chillies are added whole to sauces and dishes like risottos and then removed without eating.

Cinnamon: cinnamon sticks are added to give savoury Indian dishes a full flavour. Ground cinnamon is a popular sweet baking spice and also adds flavour to cooked fruit dishes, especially apples, rhubarb and pears.

Cloves: whole cloves are often added to Indian dishes to enhance flavour, but should be removed before serving. They can also be added to apple-based dishes. Ground cloves are usually used as a sweet baking spice.

Coriander seeds: the seeds are sold whole or ground and are used to flavour Indian and middle-eastern dishes. The flavour of coriander complements pulses and vegetable dishes.

Cumin: cumin seeds give a lovely rich flavour to savoury food and the ground seeds add earthiness to pulse dishes.

Fennel Seeds: these add a liquorice flavour to light foods and are good with vegetables such as leeks and cauliflower.

Fenugreek: the seeds are very hard, like miniature, misshapen pebbles. Available ground, this spice contributes a curry flavour to savoury dishes.

Ginger: mainly used in sweet baking, but the fresh root is added, grated, to many stir-fries and hot dishes.

Mace: the covering of the nutmeg, a net-like, golden-coloured spice available in blades or ground. Similar in flavour to nutmeg but useful as a flavouring for stocks and savoury sauces as well as vegetable or pulse dishes.

Mustard: hot and spicy to add extra interest to salad dressings and also ideal in cheese pastries, biscuits, scones and gratin dishes.

Nutmeg: mainly used grated in sweet baking recipes and in milky puddings. Also used in some savoury dishes. It is particularly good with spinach.

Paprika: prepared from dried red peppers and used to give a spicy, earthy flavour that is good with beans and other pulses. It can also be sprinkled on food as a garnish.

Saffron: expensive, natural yellow colouring which is used to colour rice dishes with a delicate golden colour. Sold as strands that must be ground before dissolving in water, then adding to the rice, or available ready powdered. Saffron has a distinctive flavour that cannot be gained from any other ingredients.

Turmeric: ground turmeric is often used to give a yellow colour. It is cheaper than saffron and is often added to recipes with other spices to give a rich balance of flavours.

SPRING

MARCH · APRIL · MAY

Towards the end of spring the new vegetables of the season start to appear in plentiful supply. The beginning of spring however sees the last of winter's stored vegetables still in the shops; produce such as swedes, turnips, parsnips, leeks, old potatoes and carrots are still good value. As the weather warms up growth speeds up in the kitchen gardens and farms and fresh produce becomes available. New carrots, turnips, sprouting broccoli, spring greens and spinach eventually make way for the first English asparagus and new potatoes. Rhubarb becomes cheaper as the season progresses and forced produce is overtaken by outdoor varieties. Most of the fruit available is imported and citrus fruits, grapes and bananas are normally good buys now. Towards the end of May home-grown fruits start appearing, gooseberries normally coming first.

SPRING MENUS

1

Citrus appetiser

Butter bean and mushroom Stroganoff with long-grain brown rice and lightly cooked carrots

Rhubarb crumble with yogurt

2

Watercress soup with wholemeal croûtons

Vegetable biriani with spiced mushrooms

Fresh fruit

3

French onion tartlets

Stir-fry vegetables with almonds and Chinese rice

Strained Greek-style natural yogurt

WATERCRESS SOUP

SERVES 4

bunch of watercress, trimmed
15 g/½ oz unsalted butter
100 g/4 oz onion, chopped
100 g/4 oz potato, scrubbed and diced
300 ml/½ pint skimmed milk
600 ml/1 pint vegetable stock
¼ teaspoon dried thyme
freshly ground black pepper

Preparation time **10 minutes**
Cooking time **40 minutes**

1 Reserve four watercress sprigs. Chop the remainder finely.
2 Melt the butter in a large saucepan and add the onion. Cook gently for 2 minutes. Stir in the watercress and potato and cook for a further 2 minutes.
3 Add remaining ingredients. Bring to the boil, reduce heat and simmer for 30 minutes.
4 Blend in a liquidiser to a purée. Reheat. Garnish with reserved watercress sprigs.

Watercress is a good source of minerals, especially of iron.

Variations
Spinach, fresh or frozen, could be used instead of the watercress. Use either 175 g/6 oz frozen or 350 g/12 oz fresh spinach. Defrost the frozen spinach, or thoroughly wash and then chop the fresh spinach, before proceeding with the recipe method as detailed. A dash of grated nutmeg can be added to the finished soup when seasoning to add extra flavour.

Garnishing Soup
A bowl of steaming hot soup makes a warm, inviting sight, but the appearance and appeal of the dish can be further enhanced with garnishing. Here are a few ideas:
* A sprinkling of fresh, chopped herbs – parsley, chives, thyme or chervil – all look attractive. Alternatively, an entire coriander leaf or small sprig of parsley can be used. A spicy soup could be garnished with a few toasted cumin seeds.
* Try adding some toasted sunflower seeds or flaked almonds.

* Use a swirl of natural yogurt for a topping lower in fat and calories than cream.
* Sprinkle on some finely chopped spring onions or finely sliced rings of raw onion.
* Add a sprinkling of cayenne, paprika or simply freshly ground black pepper.
* Reserve some finely sliced raw vegetables, like raw mushrooms or grated carrot, from cooking depending on the ingredients used in the soup.
* For a sizzling topping, heat the grill and pour the soup into ovenproof bowls. Sprinkle grated cheese on top of the soup and place under the grill to melt the cheese. This method is well known for French onion soup, but could also be used to finish off chunky vegetable soups, simple potato soups or creamy chowders. It is also ideal for transforming soups into more sustaining light meals and snacks, adding extra protein with the cheese.

Soup Accompaniments
Soup is usually served with bread to make a simple lunch or a tasty starter. The most nutritious type is wholemeal bread which has more fibre, vitamins and minerals than highly refined white bread. Wholemeal bread is widely available, sold as loaves and rolls, while keen cooks can easily make their own at home. A recipe for making basic wholemeal bread, which can be baked as loaves in many different shapes or as rolls, is contained in this section. Later in the book there are also recipes for unusual breads, made with wholemeal flour, but incorporating unusual flavourings into the dough – see Peanut butter plait (page 79) and Herb and onion twists (page 78). Bread should be served freshly baked while still warm or it can be heated through in the microwave or in the oven before serving with soup.

Sometimes the combination of soup and bread can be too filling and a lighter accompaniment is called for. Crispy croûtons of wholemeal bread are ideal. They can be prepared by toasting thinly sliced wholemeal bread and cutting it into cubes, or by lightly sautéeing cubes of wholemeal bread in sunflower oil, perhaps with the addition of some finely crushed garlic. Sprinkle croûtons on

Microwave note
Cook the onion in the butter on full power for 2 minutes. Add the potato and watercress and cook for a further 3 minutes. Add the milk and stock and cook for 12 minutes on medium power. Proceed as recipe.

top of the soup or hand separately.

Melba toast also goes well with soup. It is prepared by toasting thickly sliced wholemeal bread and then removing the crusts. Carefully cut through the centre of each slice lengthwise to make two thin pieces. Place the toast in a moderately hot oven (190 C, 375 F, gas 5) for 20 minutes and watch the toast curl up. Serve in a bread basket, fresh from the oven.

Making Stock

Stock forms the basis of most soups and is used in many other savoury dishes, such as casseroles, hot pots, sauces and risottos. Onion, celery, celeriac, leek, carrot, turnip are all ideal ingredients for stock. Avoid starchy vegetables such as potato and parsnips as these tend to make stock turn cloudy. Add a bay leaf, parsley stalks, sprig of thyme or rosemary and some black peppercorns for extra flavour. Allow 350 g/12 oz chopped vegetables to 1.4 litres/2½ pints of cold water. Place all the ingredients in a large saucepan and bring to the boil; reduce heat and cover tightly, then simmer gently for 2 hours.

Alternatively, cook the vegetables in a pressure cooker for 15 minutes at 15 lb pressure. Strain and use. Stock can be frozen for later use, in quantities of say 300 ml/½ pint or in individual cubes, prepared by freezing in ice cube trays and then storing in a plastic bag.

It is not always convenient to make stock freshly at home and there are a number of instant vegetable stock cubes or stock concentrates available. Look out for those with no artificial additives and which are low in salt.

Watercress soup

Per portion:

Calories 80

Fat 3g

Fibre 1g

Watercress soup

MUSHROOM SOUP

SERVES 4

1 tablespoon sunflower oil
100g/4oz onion, chopped
100g/4oz potato, scrubbed and diced
275g/10oz button mushrooms,
chopped
450ml/¾ pint skimmed milk
450ml/¾ pint vegetable stock
1 bay leaf
½ teaspoon dried thyme
freshly ground black pepper
chopped parsley to garnish (optional)

*Preparation time **10 minutes***
*Cooking time **40 minutes***

1 Heat the oil in a large saucepan. Stir in the onion and potato and cook over a low heat for 2 minutes without browning.
2 Add the mushrooms to the pan, stirring in well and cook for a further minute. Stir in the skimmed milk, vegetable stock, bay leaf and thyme and bring to the boil. Reduce the heat and simmer gently for 30 minutes, until the vegetables are quite soft.
3 Remove from heat and discard the bay leaf. Blend the soup in a liquidiser to a fine, smooth purée and reheat, seasoning with black pepper to taste. Serve, garnished with chopped parsley.

The skimmed milk in this recipe gives a surprisingly creamy soup but contains far fewer calories and less fat than many recipes.

Variation
Substitute a shredded leek instead of the onion to give a fuller flavour and deeper colour to the soup. Alternatively, add a crushed clove of garlic with the onion.

Microwave note
Place the oil in a casserole with the onion and potato and cook for 2 minutes on maximum power. Add the mushrooms and heat for 2 minutes. Add the milk, stock and herbs and cook for 10 minutes, stirring after 5 minutes. Proceed as recipe.

Mushroom soup

Per portion:
Calories 110
Fat 4g
Fibre 3g

SPRING VEGETABLE SOUP

SERVES 4

75g/3oz onion
100g/4oz carrots (finger carrots are ideal)
100g/4oz baby turnips
1 tablespoon sunflower oil
175g/6oz cauliflower florets
sprig of fresh thyme
1 bay leaf
900ml/1½ pints light vegetable stock
100g/4oz baby broad beans, or frozen peas, or frozen sweetcorn kernels
freshly ground black pepper
1 tablespoon chopped parsley

Mushroom soup; Spring vegetable soup

Preparation time **10 minutes**
Cooking time **30 minutes**

1 Finely chop the onion. Scrub the carrots and slice finely. Peel and dice the turnip.
2 Heat the oil in a large saucepan and add the onion. Cook for 2 minutes before stirring in the carrot, turnip and cauliflower florets. Cook for 1 minute.
3 Stir in the thyme, bay leaf and stock and bring to the boil. Add the frozen peas or sweetcorn if using. Bring to the boil and simmer for 20 minutes. Meanwhile, cook the broad beans or fresh sweetcorn kernels separately until tender and stir into the soup just before serving. Season to taste and pour into four soup bowls, garnished with freshly chopped parsley.

A light, low-calorie soup, full of fibre and vitamins and low in fat.

Variation
This soup can be prepared with a mixture of almost any fresh or frozen vegetable. Choose a colourful combination of available ingredients and cook until just tender, without becoming mushy. Try including the following vegetables to make an interesting and tasty soup – leeks, celery, green cabbage, calabrese, sprouting broccoli or potato.

Spring vegetable soup

Per portion:
Calories 65
Fat 4g
Fibre 4g

COUNTRY VEGETABLE SOUP

SERVES 4

1 tablespoon olive oil
100 g/4 oz onion, chopped
1 celery stick, chopped
100 g/4 oz potato, scrubbed and diced
100 g/4 oz carrot, scrubbed and diced
50 g/2 oz haricot beans, soaked overnight
25 g/1 oz pot or Scotch barley
1 (425-g/15-oz) can tomatoes
900 ml/1½ pints vegetable stock
1 bay leaf
¼ teaspoon marjoram
freshly ground black pepper
4 tablespoons chopped parsley to garnish

*Preparation time **10 minutes plus overnight soaking***
*Cooking time **55 minutes***

1 Heat the oil in a saucepan. Stir in the prepared vegetables and cook for 3 minutes without browning.
2 Stir in the haricot beans, pot barley, tomatoes, vegetable stock, bay leaf and marjoram and bring to the boil. Cover, reduce the heat and simmer for 50 minutes, stirring occasionally, until vegetables are soft.
3 Season with black pepper to taste. Serve in warmed soup bowls, garnished with chopped parsley.

Country vegetable soup

Per portion:	
Calories	120
Fat	4g
Fibre	5g

CARROT AND TOMATO SOUP

SERVES 3

1 tablespoon olive oil
1 clove garlic, crushed
100 g/4 oz onion, finely chopped
1 celery stick, chopped
225 g/8 oz carrots, finely diced
½ red pepper, deseeded and chopped
(optional)
1 (425-g/15-oz) can tomatoes
600 ml/1 pint vegetable stock
2 bay leaves
½ teaspoon marjoram
freshly ground black pepper
1 tablespoon chopped parsley to
garnish

Preparation time **10 minutes**
Cooking time **40 minutes**

1 Heat the oil in a saucepan. Stir in the garlic, onion, celery and carrots. Cook over a very low heat for 2 minutes without browning.
2 Add the pepper, if using, with the tomatoes, vegetable stock, bay leaves and marjoram. Bring to the boil, cover, reduce heat and simmer for 30 minutes until vegetables are soft.
3 Discard the bay leaves and blend ingredients in a liquidiser to a purée. Reheat and season with black pepper to taste. Serve garnished with chopped parsley.

This soup has a rich colour and flavour which outclasses any canned soup. It is a good source of vitamin A and is easy to reheat.

Carrot and tomato soup

Per portion:
Calories 75
Fat 5g
Fibre 3g

Freezing note
Fill a rigid plastic container with the soup leaving 2.5-cm/ 1-in headroom and freeze. Defrost the soup slowly at room temperature or in a microwave.

Country vegetable soup; Carrot and tomato soup

Russian dip and crudités

Per portion:

Calories 45

Fat 2g

Fibre 0g

Avocado dip

Per portion:

Calories 150

Fat 13g

Fibre 1g

Tahini dip

Per portion:

Calories 140

Fat 6g

Fibre 1g

Lemon dip

Per portion:

Calories 100

Fat 7g

Fibre 0g

Cucumber dip

Per portion:

Calories 45

Fat 2g

Fibre 0g

RUSSIAN DIP AND CRUDITÉS

S E R V E S   4

*100 g/4 oz low-fat soft cheese
4 tablespoons strained, Greek-style
natural yogurt
1 clove garlic, crushed
1 tablespoon tomato purée
dash of Tabasco or Worcestershire
sauce
freshly ground black pepper*
To serve
*carrots, cauliflower, peppers,
cucumber, celery*

Preparation time **15 minutes,
plus 4 hours, or overnight, to chill**

1 Place the cheese in a bowl. Carefully stir in the yogurt, garlic, tomato purée and chosen sauce. Season with pepper. Cover tightly and leave to chill in the refrigerator for several hours, or overnight.
2 Just before serving prepare the vegetables. Scrub the carrots and cut into fairly thick strips. Divide the cauliflower into florets, deseed the peppers and cut into fine strips, cut the cucumber and celery into strips.
3 Serve the crudités with the dip.

Choose a low-fat soft cheese such as continental quark as the base for the dip.

Variations
Avocado Dip
Purée two ripe avocados and add the soft cheese and yogurt. Replace the garlic, tomato purée and Tabasco with the juice of half a lemon.

Tahini Dip
Use 225 g/8 oz set yogurt puréed with 4 tablespoons tahini (sesame seed paste), instead of the soft cheese. Add 2 tablespoons lemon juice, $\frac{1}{2}$ teaspoon chilli powder and 1 crushed clove garlic, but omit the tomato purée and Tabasco.

Lemon Dip
Omit the tomato purée and Tabasco from the dip and add 2 finely chopped spring onions, 2 tablespoons mayonnaise and the juice of half a lemon.

Cucumber dip
Add half a cucumber, peeled, deseeded and finely chopped to the soft cheese and yogurt, and garlic, but leave out the tomato purée and Tabasco seasonings.

Crudités
Presentation is the key to the success of dips and crudités. Choose a colourful selection of top quality fresh produce, prepare and then cut into even lengths for serving. Carrots, celery, cucumber, red, green, yellow (and even black) peppers, courgettes and spring onions are some of the best vegetables to use. Tiny button mushrooms, carefully washed and also small cauliflower florets can be served as crudités.

Crisp savoury finger biscuits are tasty eaten with dips. Twiglets are good for dipping and are surprisingly healthy as they are baked from wholemeal flour and yeast extract. Cheese biscuits are

also suitable. They can be prepared by rolling out thinly and cutting into long thin 'straws' (see Cheese Biscuit recipe on page 157).

CITRUS APPETISER

SERVES 4

2 large oranges · 1 grapefruit
1 ugli fruit · juice of 1 lime
1 tablespoon Cointreau (optional)

Preparation time **15 minutes, plus 30 minutes to chill**

1 Pare the rind from one orange.
2 Peel the oranges, grapefruit and ugli fruit and remove pith. Cut into 2.5-cm/1-in lengths and toss together in the lime juice with the Cointreau, if using. Sprinkle with the pared orange rind. Chill for 30 minutes and serve.

Citrus fruits are good value during spring and boost supplies of home-grown fruits, supplying valuable vitamin C.

Variation
Melon Refresher
Omit the ugli fruit and use a small Galia melon, peeled, deseeded and cut into small chunks.

Nutty Touch
If liked, garnish the dishes just before serving with 50g/2oz lightly toasted pine kernels and 25g/1oz lightly toasted flaked almonds. This adds an interesting, crunchy topping to the dish.

Russian dip and crudités; Citrus appetiser

Citrus appetiser	
Per portion:	
Calories 60	
Fat trace	
Fibre 2g	

Nutty touch	
Per portion:	
Calories 180	
Fat 8g	
Fibre 4g	

MUSHROOM SOUFFLÉ QUICHE

SERVES 4

Oat Pastry
75 g/3 oz plain wholemeal flour
25 g/1 oz rolled oats
50 g/2 oz soft vegetable margarine
Filling
1 tablespoon olive oil
50 g/2 oz onion, finely chopped
½ red pepper, deseeded and chopped
100 g/4 oz mushrooms, finely chopped
¼ teaspoon dried thyme
2 free-range eggs, separated
100 g/4 oz low-fat soft cheese
2 tablespoons chopped parsley
25 g/1 oz Cheddar cheese, finely grated
freshly ground black pepper

Preparation time **20 minutes plus 15 minutes to chill**
Cooking time **45 minutes**
Oven temperature **200 C, 400 F, gas 6**
190 C, 375 F, gas 5

1 Place the flour in a bowl with the oats and rub in the margarine until the mixture resembles fine breadcrumbs. Chill for 15 minutes.
2 Start preparing the filling. Heat the oil in a saucepan and cook the onion and pepper gently for 2 minutes. Add the mushrooms and cook for a further 3 minutes to let the juices run, then add the thyme.
3 Keep the separated egg whites in a bowl in the refrigerator. Mix the egg yolks with the soft cheese, then beat in the mushroom mixture. Add the parsley and grated Cheddar. Season with pepper and set aside.
4 Add just enough cold water to the flour mixture to make a smooth dough. Roll out the pastry and line an 18-cm/7-in flan ring or dish. Bake blind for 10 minutes, remove paper and bake for a further 5 minutes, then reduce the heat.
5 Stiffly whisk the egg whites and fold into the mushroom mixture. Place in the pastry case and bake for 20–25 minutes until the quiche is well-risen and golden brown.

The addition of oats to the pastry gives an extra nutty flavour. The filling soon sinks, so serve the dish straight from the oven.

INDIAN CAULIFLOWER

SERVES 4

2 tablespoons sunflower oil
175 g/6 oz onion, finely chopped
1 clove garlic, crushed
1 fresh green chilli, deseeded and chopped
½ teaspoon turmeric
½ teaspoon ground cumin
1 teaspoon ground coriander
175 g/6 oz tomatoes, chopped
1 large cauliflower, divided into florets
3 tablespoons water
1 teaspoon garam masala

Preparation time **10 minutes**
Cooking time **30 minutes**

1 Heat the oil in a saucepan. Add the onion, garlic and chilli and cook for 3 minutes over a low heat without browning.
2 Stir in the turmeric, cumin and coriander and cook for another minute. Add the tomatoes and cook for 5 minutes.
3 Stir in the cauliflower florets and mix with the other ingredients. Add the water, cover and simmer gently for 20 minutes or until the cauliflower is tender. Check to make sure that the cauliflower does not dry up during cooking. The cooked vegetable should be moist without excess cooking liquid.
4 Turn off the heat, but leave saucepan on the hob. Stir in the garam masala and leave to stand for 5 minutes.

This spicy vegetable mixture is ideal to serve with Vegetable Biriani (see page 33) but omit the cauliflower from the recipe.

Mushroom soufflé quiche

Per portion:	
Calories	310
Fat	20g
Fibre	3g

Indian cauliflower

Per portion:	
Calories	100
Fat	7g
Fibre	4g

Mushroom soufflé quiche; Indian cauliflower

LASAGNE BAKE

SERVES 4

10 pieces wholemeal lasagne
100 g/4 oz onion, chopped
2 cloves garlic, crushed
1 tablespoon olive oil
175 g/6 oz carrots, finely diced
450 g/1 lb tomatoes, peeled and
chopped
$\frac{1}{2}$ teaspoon dried or 1 teaspoon
chopped fresh basil
1 red pepper, deseeded and chopped
1 bay leaf
450 g/1 lb spinach
25 g/1 oz soft vegetable margarine
25 g/1 oz plain wholemeal flour
300 ml/$\frac{1}{2}$ pint skimmed milk
50 g/2 oz Cheddar cheese, finely
grated, plus 15 g/$\frac{1}{2}$ oz
freshly ground black pepper

Preparation time **35–40 minutes**
Cooking time **1 hour 10 minutes**
Oven temperature **190 C, 375 F, gas 5**

Microwave note

The tomato sauce, cheese sauce and spinach can all be cooked in the microwave oven to save time. The tomato sauce will need 8 minutes further cooking on full power after the onion, garlic and carrots have been cooked in the oil for 2 minutes on full power. The spinach will need 5–6 minutes in a roasting bag on full power and the cheese sauce can be prepared by melting the margarine on full power, stirring in the flour and cooking in the oven for 1 minute. Heat the milk for 2 minutes, then beat into the flour and margarine mixture. Cook for 2 minutes, stir in the cheese and pepper and cook for 1 further minute. The assembled lasagne could then be cooked on full power for 8 minutes.

1 Cook the lasagne by plunging the sheets into a pan of fast boiling water. Cook for 10–12 minutes until *al dente* (almost tender). Drain well.

2 Make a tomato sauce. Cook the onion and garlic gently in the oil for 2 minutes. Add the carrots, tomatoes, basil, pepper and bay leaf. Bring to the boil, then reduce the heat and simmer for 25 minutes.

3 Meanwhile, cook the spinach and chop finely, draining out surplus fluid.

4 Make a cheese sauce. Melt the margarine in a pan. Stir in the flour and cook for 1 minute, before gradually adding the milk. Bring to the boil, stirring continuously to make a smooth sauce. Add the 50 g/2 oz of Cheddar and season with black pepper.

5 Assemble the lasagne in a lightly oiled oblong ovenproof dish by placing a layer of lasagne in the base and adding layers of tomato sauce, lasagne, spinach, tomato sauce and lasagne and finally topping with cheese sauce. Sprinkle with the remaining cheese and bake for 35 minutes or until brown and bubbling. Serve with green vegetables or a side salad.

Wholemeal lasagne is higher in fibre and B vitamins than traditional white lasagne. Layer this tasty and nutritious pasta with iron-rich spinach instead of meat.

LENTIL SAUCE

SERVES 4

100 g / 4 oz onion, chopped
2 celery sticks, sliced
2 cloves garlic, crushed
1 tablespoon olive oil
225 g / 8 oz button mushrooms, sliced
1 red pepper, deseeded and chopped
1 green pepper, deseeded and chopped
200 g / 7 oz red lentils
1 (425-g / 15-oz) can or 450 g / 1 lb fresh tomatoes, peeled and chopped
½ teaspoon dried basil
2 bay leaves
300 ml / ½ pint dry red wine or vegetable stock
2 tablespoons tomato purée
freshly ground black pepper
grated Parmesan cheese
chopped parsley to garnish

Preparation time **15 minutes**
Cooking time **45 minutes**

1 Cook the onion, celery and garlic in the oil for 2 minutes without browning.
2 Stir in the mushrooms, peppers, lentils, tomatoes, basil, bay leaves, wine or stock and tomato purée. Bring to the boil, then reduce the heat, cover and simmer gently for 40 minutes, stirring occasionally to make sure the sauce does not stick; add a little extra stock if it begins to dry out. Season with freshly ground black pepper and serve stirred into cooked long-grain brown rice. Sprinkle over the Parmesan and garnish with parsley.

A super vegetarian alternative to a traditional meat-based sauce. This can also be served with wholemeal spaghetti, or used as an alternative to the sauce in Lasagne bake. Red wine gives a lovely rich flavour, but vegetable stock can be used in its place if preferred.

Microwave note
The sauce can be cooked in the microwave. Cook the garlic, onion and celery in the oil for 1 minute on full power. Add the remaining ingredients, cover and cook for 15 minutes on full power. Stir and cook for a further 15 minutes until the lentils are fully soft.

Lasagne bake	
Per portion:	
Calories 490	
Fat 12g	
Fibre 17g	

Lentil sauce	
Per portion:	
Calories 400	
Fat 7g	
Fibre 9g	

Lasagne bake; Lentil sauce with rice

SPINACH-STUFFED PANCAKES

SERVES 4

Stuffing
450 g / 1 lb spinach
100 g / 4 oz low-fat soft cheese
50 g / 2 oz onion, chopped
15 g / ½ oz butter or 1 teaspoon sunflower oil
pinch of grated nutmeg
freshly ground black pepper
Batter
100 g / 4 oz plain wholemeal flour
1 free-range egg
300 ml / ½ pint skimmed milk
vegetable oil
75 g / 3 oz toasted split almonds to garnish

Preparation time **15 minutes**
Cooking time **25–30 minutes**

1 Wash the spinach thoroughly, discarding any coarse stalks and yellowing leaves. Place in a saucepan and cook covered over a low heat for 5–8 minutes until soft. Drain thoroughly and chop. Mix with the cheese.
2 Soften the onion in the butter or oil for 2 minutes. Mix into the spinach and cheese mixture with the nutmeg and enough pepper to taste.
3 Make the pancakes. Sift the flour, adding any bran remaining in the sieve. Make a well in the centre and add the egg. Gradually mix in the flour, beating in half of the milk. Continue beating until really smooth. Mix in the remaining milk.
4 Heat a little oil in an 18-cm / 7-in crêpe pan. Tip in just enough mixture to coat the base of the pan and cook gently until set. Toss or turn to cook the other side. Cook all the batter in this way, keeping the pancakes hot on a plate.
5 When all the batter has been used, place some of the spinach mixture in the centre of each pancake and fold or roll up. Place on an ovenproof plate and reheat all the pancakes together, either by placing, covered, in a moderate oven (180 C, 350 F, gas 4), or in a microwave on full power for 4 minutes.
6 Just before serving, sprinkle with the toasted amonds.

Pancakes can be made successfully with wholemeal flour and give a surprisingly light result. They make a useful 'container' for a savoury stuffing, such as this nutritious stuffing of spinach and low-fat soft cheese.

SPICED MUSHROOMS

SERVES 4

1 tablespoon sunflower oil
½ teaspoon ground coriander
½ teaspoon ground cumin
¼ teaspoon chilli powder (or half a fresh chilli, deseeded and chopped)
¼ teaspoon cayenne
¼ teaspoon turmeric
100 g / 4 oz onion, chopped
2 cloves garlic, crushed
1 cm / ½ in fresh root ginger, peeled and grated
350 g / 12 oz button mushrooms
1 (425-g / 15-oz) can or 450 g / 1 lb fresh tomatoes, peeled and chopped

Preparation time **10 minutes**
Cooking time **30 minutes**

1 Heat the oil and add the spices, onion, garlic and ginger. Cook for 2 minutes, then stir in the mushrooms and tomatoes. Bring to the boil, cover and simmer for 20 minutes. Serve hot.

A delicious accompaniment to Vegetable biriani.

Freezing note
Ready-made pancakes can be frozen for later use. Place each pancake on a layer of greaseproof paper and stack up. Place in a polythene bag and freeze.

Spinach-stuffed pancakes

Per portion:	
Calories	320
Fat	17g
Fibre	7g

Spiced mushrooms

Per portion:

Calories 70

Fat 4g

Fibre 4g

*Spiced mushrooms;
Spinach-stuffed
pancakes*

27

Microwave note
It is possible to stir-fry in the microwave by using a preheated browning dish to start the dish off and cooking on full power until the vegetables are tender.

Stir-fry vegetables with almonds

Per portion:

Calories 210

Fat 17g

Fibre 8g

STIR-FRY VEGETABLES WITH ALMONDS

SERVES 4

2 leeks
100g/4oz carrots, scrubbed
100g/4oz swede, peeled
1 tablespoon sesame oil
2 cloves garlic, crushed
50g/2oz mushrooms, sliced
75g/3oz curly kale or other dark green leafy vegetable, shredded
1 tablespoon soy sauce
1 tablespoon dry sherry or rice wine
4 tablespoons water
225g/8oz mung beanshoots
100g/4oz split almonds, toasted

*Preparation time **25 minutes***
*Cooking time **7 minutes***

1 Trim away the coarse leaves and roots from the leeks, clean carefully and chop the leeks finely. Cut the carrots and swede into 2.5–5-cm/1–2-in long matchsticks.
2 Heat the oil in a wok or large heavy-based frying pan. Add the garlic, leek, carrot and swede. Cook for 3 minutes, stirring often. Add the mushrooms and kale and cook for 1 minute. Add the soy sauce, sherry or rice wine, water and beanshoots. Cook for 3 minutes. Add the almonds and serve.

Stir-frying is a quick method of cooking which helps to retain nutritional value. If you do not own a wok, a large heavy-based frying pan will do just as well.

Variations
Almost any combination of vegetables can be used in this dish. Choose ingredients that make a colourful mixture and which give various textures. Try adding the following combinations of ingredients to make delicious stir-fries.

Celery and parsnip stir-fry: *add parsnips and celery instead of the carrots and swede.*

Broccoli and waterchestnut stir-fry: *use broccoli spears instead of the curly kale and add sliced waterchestnuts (available canned) instead of the swede.*

Courgette and pepper stir-fry: *use sliced courgettes instead of the curly kale and add strips of red, green or yellow pepper instead of the swede.*

Cashew nut stir-fry: *substitute cashew nuts for the almonds.*

Tofu stir-fry: *add small cubes of tofu to the stir-fry instead of the nuts.*

CHINESE RICE

SERVES 4

225g/8oz long-grain brown rice, cooked and cooled
1 tablespoon sesame oil
100g/4oz mushrooms, finely sliced
100g/4oz beanshoots
1 large free-range egg

*Preparation time **5 minutes***
*Cooking time **10 minutes***

1 The rice should be completely cool for this dish, so refrigerate until required. Separate the grains.
2 Heat the oil in a wok or large, heavy-based frying pan and add the rice. Stir in thoroughly and cook for 4 minutes.
3 Add the mushrooms and beanshoots and cook for a further 2 minutes.
4 Add the egg, stirring constantly to break it up as it sets. Continue cooking until it has set, then serve at once.

Mushrooms and beanshoots are available all the year round; neither depends on the vagaries of the climate for growth as each is raised under cover.

Variations
An alternative method of preparing fried rice is to proceed as in the main recipe but to substitute hard-boiled egg instead of uncooked egg. Cook the rice as detailed but when the egg should be

added continue cooking without. Arrange the cooked rice on a serving dish and place a ring of sliced hard-boiled egg around the edge as a garnish. Finish with a little finely shredded lettuce and serve.

This dish can also be prepared with a colourful mixture of vegetables instead of the mushrooms and beanshoots. Try some of the following combinations.

Broccoli and red pepper: add diced pepper and small broccoli spears, then mix in a few chopped spring onions just before serving.

Spinach and beanshoots: use shredded spinach instead of the mushrooms and sprinkle in some chopped spring onions. Follow the above suggestion for using hard-boiled eggs.

Leek and carrot: use sliced leeks instead of the mushrooms and add matchstick strips of new carrots instead of the beanshoots.

Spring cabbage and tofu: use finely shredded spring cabbage instead of the beanshoots. Add small cubes of tofu instead of the egg.

Peas and beanshoots: substitute peas for the mushrooms. Most types of beanshoots can be used instead of mung beanshoots but alfalfa seeds are too fine.

Stir-fry vegetables with almonds; Chinese rice

Chinese rice	
Per portion:	
Calories 270	
Fat 6g	
Fibre 4g	

FRENCH ONION TARTLETS

SERVES 4

175 g/6 oz plain wholemeal flour
75 g/3 oz soft vegetable margarine
generous pinch of mustard powder
cold water to mix
Filling
175 g/6 oz onion
15 g/½ oz butter or soft vegetable margarine
175 g/6 oz low-fat soft cheese
1 free-range egg
4 tablespoons skimmed milk
¼ teaspoon mustard powder
freshly ground black pepper
40 g/1½ oz farmhouse Cheddar, finely grated
chopped chives to garnish

Preparation time **10–15 minutes, plus 15 minutes to chill**
Cooking time **30 minutes**
Oven temperature **200 C, 400 F, gas 6**

---

1 Sift the flour into a bowl and add the bran from the sieve. Rub in the margarine and stir in the mustard. Chill for 15 minutes. Add just sufficient cold water to mix to a soft dough and roll out the pastry

French onion tartlet

to line four 10-cm/4-in tartlet tins. Bake blind (place a piece of greaseproof paper over the pastry and sprinkle over a few dried beans to prevent pastry bubbling up) for 10 minutes.
2 Very finely chop the onion and cook gently in the butter or margarine without browning, until soft.
3 Beat together the soft cheese, egg, milk, mustard and freshly ground black pepper.
4 Remove the paper from the tartlet tins and divide the onion between the four tartlets. Pour over the beaten cheese mixture and sprinkle the grated Cheddar on top. Bake for 20 minutes and serve immediately while the tartlets are still light and fluffy. Garnish with chopped chives and serve with a light salad – finely shredded lettuce or Chinese leaves with finely shredded radicchio, form an attractive combination.

A tasty hot starter, lower in calories than many conventional quiche recipes as low-fat soft cheese replaces the cream often used.

WALNUT AND SOFT CHEESE TAGLIATELLE

SERVES 4

25 g/1 oz unsalted butter
100 g/4 oz onion, chopped
225 g/8 oz quark or similar low-fat soft cheese
6 tablespoons strained, Greek-style natural yogurt
1 tablespoon chopped fresh chives
freshly ground black pepper
350 g/12 oz wholemeal tagliatelle
100 g/4 oz walnut halves
1 tablespoon chopped fresh chives to garnish

Preparation time **10 minutes**
Cooking time **10–20 minutes**

---

1 Heat the butter and stir in the onion. Cook over a low heat for 4 minutes.
2 Remove from heat and stir in the quark or soft cheese, yogurt and chives, then season with pepper.

Microwave note
At stage 2 cook the onions in the butter or margarine on full power for 3 minutes until soft.

French onion tartlets

Per portion:

Calories 420

Fat 25g

Fibre 5g

Microwave note
For Walnut and soft cheese tagliatelle melt the butter in a covered dish on maximum power for 1 minute. Stir in the onions and cook for 2 minutes. Proceed as recipe.

Walnut and soft cheese tagliatelle

Per portion:
Calories 580
Fat 22g
Fibre 10g

Walnut and soft cheese tagliatelle

3 Cook the tagliatelle in plenty of boiling water for a couple of minutes, if using fresh pasta, or for 12–15 minutes if using dried pasta. Drain and return to the pan, stirring in the sauce and walnut halves. Heat through for a couple of minutes and serve, garnished with chopped chives.

Use a soft, low-fat cheese in preference to fat-rich and calorie-laden cream cheeses in this speedy supper dish. Butter gives a richer taste to the sauce, but if preferred a vegetable oil could be used in its place.

Microwave note

At stage 2, heat the onion on full power for 2 minutes. Add the mushrooms, cook for 1 minute. Add the flour and cook for 1 minute. Heat the milk with the stock, then beat into the mushroom mixture to form a smooth sauce. Cook for 2 minutes, stir in the butter beans, and reheat for 1 minute when the rice is ready. Stir in the yogurt and season to taste. Sprinkle with parsley.

Butter bean and mushroom Stroganoff; Vegetable biriani

Butter bean and mushroom Stroganoff

Per portion:	
Calories	280
Fat	9g
Fibre	15g

BUTTER BEAN AND MUSHROOM STROGANOFF

SERVES 4

*225 g | 8 oz butter beans, soaked overnight
1 small onion, chopped
2 tablespoons sunflower oil
350 g | 12 oz button mushrooms, halved
2 tablespoons wholemeal flour
175 ml | 6 fl oz skimmed milk
175 ml | 6 fl oz vegetable stock
$\frac{1}{4}$ teaspoon dried thyme
freshly ground black pepper
3 tablespoons natural yogurt
chopped parsley to garnish*

Preparation time **10 minutes, plus overnight soaking**
Cooking time **1 hour 25 minutes**

1 Drain the beans and place in a pan of cold water and cook for 1–1$\frac{1}{4}$ hours or until quite tender.
2 Cook the onion in the oil for 2 minutes.
3 Add the mushrooms to the onion. Cook gently for 2 minutes. Stir in the flour and cook for 1 minute. Gradually add the milk and stock, stirring continuously to make a smooth sauce. Stir in the thyme and season to taste.
4 Add the drained butter beans and reheat. Stir in the yogurt just before serving and sprinkle with the chopped parsley.

A delicious and creamy supper dish, served with boiled, long-grain brown rice for a perfectly balanced protein intake.

1 Heat the oil in a large saucepan and add the cumin seeds. Let them sizzle for a few seconds, then add and cook the onion, garlic, potatoes and carrots gently together for 2 minutes.

2 Add the turmeric and ground cumin and stir in well. Add the cauliflower florets and stir in. Now add the rice, mixing in the spice mixture thoroughly. Let this cook for 1 minute before adding the stock and bay leaf. Bring to the boil, then reduce the heat and simmer for 25 minutes.

3 Toast the cashew nuts and almonds and have ready. Test the rice; if it is tender and all the stock is absorbed, then add the nuts and serve. If some stock still remains in the pan, then turn up the heat and cook uncovered for a while to evaporate the stock. Stir in the nuts and pepper to taste.

A tasty way of livening up vegetables. The nuts complement the protein in the brown rice and add a delicious flavour too. Serve with Spiced mushrooms (see page 18) and some crunchy poppadums for a spicy Indian supper.

Microwave note
Cooking brown rice in a microwave does not save much time, but the microwave is invaluable in reheating cooked rice dishes such as this vegetable biriani. Either reheat the whole amount for 4–5 minutes, or serve on plates and reheat for a couple of minutes.

Vegetable biriani

Per portion:
Calories **490**
Fat **16g**
Fibre **10g**

VEGETABLE BIRIANI

SERVES 4

1 tablespoon sesame oil
$\frac{1}{2}$ teaspoon cumin seeds
100g/4oz onion, chopped
1 clove garlic, crushed
225g/8oz potatoes, scrubbed and diced
225g/8oz carrots, scrubbed and diced
$\frac{1}{2}$ teaspoon turmeric
$\frac{1}{2}$ teaspoon ground cumin
225g/8oz cauliflower florets
275g/10oz long-grain brown rice
750ml/1$\frac{1}{4}$ pints vegetable stock
1 bay leaf
50g/2oz cashew nuts
50g/2oz split almonds
freshly ground black pepper

Preparation time **15 minutes**
Cooking time **30 minutes**

Freezing and Microwave note

Freeze after cooking by arranging each burger on a piece of foil and covering well. Defrost in the microwave on defrost setting for 4 minutes. Then heat through at full power for 3 minutes.

Cheese and rice burgers; Rhubarb crumble

CHEESE AND RICE BURGERS

SERVES 4

75g/3oz Cheddar with onion and herbs, finely grated
75g/3oz long-grain brown rice, cooked and cooled
generous pinch of mustard powder
2 free-range eggs
4 tablespoons medium oatmeal
2 tablespoons oil
Garnish
grated carrot
watercress sprigs
tomato wedges

*Preparation time **20 minutes, plus 10 minutes to chill***
*Cooking time **6 minutes***

1 Place the cheese in a mixing bowl. Stir in the rice and mustard and mix together thoroughly.
2 Beat one of the eggs and add enough to the mixture to bind it together. Shape into four burgers and chill for 10 minutes.
3 Beat the remaining egg and mix with any leftover mixture. Place in a shallow bowl. Place the oatmeal in a second bowl. One by one coat each burger first in the egg and then the oatmeal, shaking off any excess. Place on a plate and chill for a further 10 minutes.
4 Heat a little oil in a frying pan and fry each burger for 3 minutes on each side. Shake off any excess oil and serve with grated carrot, watercress sprigs and tomato wedges.

Good hot or cold, these are a tasty snack and useful for the packed lunch box too. If preferred, a plain Cheddar cheese could be used in place of the Cheddar with onion and herbs, but the latter gives an interesting flavour.

RHUBARB CRUMBLE

SERVES 4

100g/4oz plain wholemeal flour
50g/2oz rolled oats
65g/2½oz soft vegetable margarine
50g/2oz raw cane demerara sugar
pinch of ground cinnamon
575g/1¼lb rhubarb
1 piece preserved stem ginger in honey, diced
1 tablespoon clear honey
1 tablespoon water

*Preparation time **25 minutes***
*Cooking time **30 minutes***
*Oven temperature **200 C, 400 F, gas 6***

1 Place the flour and oats in a mixing bowl and rub in the margarine until the consistency is fine. Stir in sugar and cinnamon.
2 Trim the rhubarb and remove any coarse stringy pieces. Cut into 1-cm/½-in lengths. Place the ginger with the rhubarb in the bottom of a deep ovenproof dish. Drizzle the honey and water over and top with the crumble mixture.
3 Bake for 25–30 minutes until the fruit is soft and the topping golden brown. Serve hot or cold with natural yogurt.

Rhubarb is low in calories, high in fibre.

Freezing note
Freeze the uncooked crumble but cover the pie dish with foil and wrap in a polythene bag. Cook from frozen as above, but allow an extra 5 minutes cooking time at a lower heat.

Cheese and rice burgers

Per portion:

Calories 310

Fat 18g

Fibre 2g

Rhubarb crumble

Per portion:

Calories 270

Fat 15g

Fibre 7g

Microwave note
Dried apricots can be cooked quickly in the microwave. Take 100 g/4 oz dried apricots and place them in an ovenproof basin. Just cover with cold water and cook on full power for 8 minutes.

Caribbean fruit cocktail	
Per portion:	
Calories 120	
Fat 0g	
Fibre 4g	

CARIBBEAN FRUIT COCKTAIL

SERVES 6

1 mango
1 guava
$\frac{1}{2}$ galia melon or $\frac{1}{4}$ honeydew melon
1 orange
2 pieces preserved stem ginger
2 kiwi fruit
1 tablespoon white rum (optional)
3 tablespoons orange juice
1 large banana
25 g/ 1 oz fresh coconut, coarsely grated

---

*Preparation time **25 minutes plus 1 hour to chill***

---

1 Peel the mango, holding it over a dish to catch any juice. Cut all the flesh away from the stone and chop fairly finely. Reserve all the juice to add to the salad. Halve the guava, cut into quarters and dice. Cut away the melon flesh from the peel and chop. Remove the peel from the orange and cut into horizontal slices. Chop each slice into 4.

2 Place all the prepared fruit and juice in a large serving dish. Mix together. Thinly slice the ginger and add to the cocktail. Peel the kiwi fruit and slice. Cut each slice in half and add to the bowl.

3 Pour over the white rum, if using, and add the orange juice.

4 Cover the dish and leave to chill for at least one hour. Just before serving, slice the banana finely and add to the bowl. Sprinkle with the fresh coconut. Serve with yogurt.

During the winter and spring, exotic fruits from abroad are often good value and make up for the shortage of home-grown fresh fruits.

*Caribbean fruit cocktail;
Apricot fluff*

APRICOT FLUFF

SERVES 4

*100 g/4 oz dried apricots, soaked
overnight
1 (225-g/8-oz) pot of strained Greek
yogurt
25 g/1 oz flaked almonds*

*Preparation time **10 minutes, plus
overnight soaking**
Cooking time **25 minutes***

1 Place the apricots and their water in a saucepan and heat until boiling. Reduce heat and simmer for 20 minutes until tender. Drain, but reserve liquid.
2 Blend the apricots in a liquidiser with 3 tablespoons reserved liquid to a smooth purée. Cool.
3 Beat the purée into the yogurt and then divide between 4 serving glasses.

4 Lightly toast the almonds under a hot grill and scatter over the serving glasses.

Dried apricots are a useful store-cupboard standby; they are also a good source of vitamin A and iron.

Apricot fluff
Per portion:
Calories 160
Fat 7g
Fibre 7g

Microwave note
Make up the reserved fruit juice to 450 ml/¾ pint with orange juice and add in the Gelozone. Heat on half power for 2 minutes, then stir well. Heat for a further 2 minutes to thicken.

Trifle	
Whole recipe:	
Calories 1,820	
Fat 95g	
Fibre 12g	

TRIFLE

SERVES 6

Sponge
50 g/2 oz soft vegetable margarine
50 g/2 oz light muscovado sugar
1 free-range egg
50 g/2 oz plain wholemeal flour
1 teaspoon baking powder
1 tablespoon no-added-sugar apricot jam
1 tablespoon dry sherry (optional)
2 tablespoon orange juice
Fruit filling
orange juice to make up juice to 450 ml/¾ pint
1 (425-g/15-oz) can peaches
1 (200-g/7-oz) can pears in natural juice
2 teaspoons Gelozone
Custard
2 free-range eggs
2 free-range egg yolks
1 tablespoon light muscovado sugar
300 ml/½ pint skimmed milk
Decoration
50 g/2 oz toasted flaked almonds

Preparation time **30 minutes plus 1 hour to set**
Cooking time **25 minutes**
Oven temperature **180 C, 350 F, gas 4**

1 To make the sponge, cream together the margarine and sugar until light and fluffy. Beat in the egg.
2 Sift together the flour and baking powder and fold in and mix well. Smooth the mixture into a greased and lined 18-cm/7-in sandwich tin and bake for 20 minutes until light and risen, and just firm to the touch.
3 Remove from tin and cool on a wire rack.
4 Cut the sponge in half and spread with the jam. Cut into small pieces and line the base of a glass serving dish. If using, pour sherry over and add 2 tablespoons of orange juice. Drain the canned fruit, reserving the juice.
5 Chop the fruit and arrange on top of the sponge. Make up the juices to 450 ml/¾ pint with extra orange juice.
6 Beat the Gelozone into the juice and place in a saucepan and heat gently,

stirring constantly to thicken the mixture. Immediately pour onto the fruit and leave to set for a few minutes.
7 When the jelly has set, make the custard. Whisk together the eggs, egg yolks and sugar in a jug. Heat the milk in a saucepan but do not allow to boil. Pour over the egg mixture and stir well.
8 Stand the jug in a saucepan of hot water or use a double boiler, to gently bring the custard to setting point, without allowing it to boil. Stir constantly until the custard is thick enough to coat the back of a spoon. The custard must be thickened enough to set but do not allow it to boil or it will curdle.
9 Pour over the jelly and leave to set for 1 hour. Decorate when quite cold with almonds and serve.
Home-made custard is used for extra flavour instead of instant custard in this recipe. Gelatine can be used in place of the vegetarian setting agent, Gelozone. Simply dissolve the gelatine in a small amount of juice, then add to the remaining juice. The sponge could be made in advance and frozen down.

Variations
Mandarin Pear Trifle
Tangy mandarin oranges and fresh pears mingle with carob-flavoured sponge cake and custard to make an exciting new trifle. Add 1 tablespoon carob powder to the sponge cake, mixing it in with the wholemeal flour.

For the fruit filling, use 1 (280-g/9-oz) can mandarin oranges in natural juice. Peel, core and slice 4 ripe pears and dip them in a little lemon juice. Make up the fruit filling as in the main recipe, reserving a few mandarin oranges and a few pear slices for the decoration.

Flavour the custard by whisking in 1 tablespoon carob powder with the egg mixture. Build up the layers in the trifle as for the main recipe, then decorate the top with the reserved fruit and some flaked almonds.

Apricot Almond Trifle
Lightly flavoured almond sponge can be used as a base for an apricot trifle. Add 25 g/1 oz ground almonds to the sponge cake, mixing it in with the flour.

For the fruit filling use 2 (411-g/14½-oz) cans apricots in natural juice and make up the filling as in the main recipe.

Mandarin pear trifle

Whole recipe:

Calories 2160

Fat 95g

Fibre 21g

Apricot almond trifle

Whole recipe:

Calories 2210

Fat 109g

Fibre 24g

Trifle

Coarsely grate the rind from 2 oranges and add most of it to the prepared custard, reserving a little for decoration. Top the trifle with the custard as in the main recipe.

Cut all the pith from the oranges, slice the fruit and dicard the pips. Arrange the slices on top of the trifle and decorate with the reserved grated orange rind. It is best to add the fresh orange decoration a short while before the trifle is to be served.

Bakewell tart
Per portion:
Calories 320
Fat 20g
Fibre 4g

Flapjacks
Per portion:
Calories 100–130
Fat 3–4g
Fibre 1–2g

BAKEWELL TART

SERVES 6

100 g/4 oz plain wholemeal flour
50 g/2 oz soft vegetable margarine
Topping
3 tablespoons no-added-sugar
strawberry or raspberry jam
50 g/2 oz soft vegetable margarine
50 g/2 oz muscovado sugar
1 free-range egg
50 g/2 oz wholemeal flour
25 g/1 oz ground almonds
$\frac{1}{2}$ teaspoon baking powder
1–2 tablespoons skimmed milk
25 g/1 oz flaked almonds to decorate

Preparation time **20 minutes plus 15
minutes to chill**
Cooking time **25 minutes**
Oven temperature **190 C, 375 F, gas 5**

1 Place the flour in a mixing bowl and
rub in the margarine until mixture
resembles fine breadcrumbs. Chill for
10–15 minutes. Then add just enough
cold water to mix to a soft dough. Roll
out on a lightly floured surface to a
circle just large enough to line an
18-cm/7-in fluted flan dish. Reserve any
pastry trimmings.
2 Spread the jam inside the flan case.
Place the margarine and sugar in a bowl
and cream together until light and
fluffy. Beat in the egg, then fold in the
flour, ground almonds and baking powder, adding enough milk to give a
smooth textured mixture. Spread
evenly on top of the jam.
3 Roll out the pastry trimmings and cut
into fine strips, twist and then arrange
on top of the tart in a lattice. Sprinkle
the flaked almonds on top.
4 Glaze the pastry with a little milk and
then bake for 20–25 minutes until
golden brown in colour and firm to the
touch.

An old family favourite is given the
'wholemeal' treatment in this tasty
recipe which is equally good hot or cold.

FLAPJACKS

MAKES 8–10 SLICES

175 g/6 oz rolled oats
25 g/1 oz desiccated coconut
2 tablespoons sesame seeds
75 g/3 oz soft vegetable margarine
2 tablespoons malt extract and
1 tablespoon clear honey
or alternatively use 3 tablespoons
clear honey

Preparation time **10 minutes**
Cooking time **30 minutes**
Oven temperature **180 C, 350 F, gas 4**

1 Mix the oats, coconut and sesame
seeds together.
2 Heat the margarine with the malt
extract and honey until the margarine
has melted. Remove from the heat and
stir in the oats mixture.
3 Press firmly into a lightly greased
18-cm/7-in square sandwich tin and
bake in the centre of the oven for 20–25
minutes until golden brown.
4 Mark the flapjacks into fingers but
leave to cool in the tin.

Adding sesame seeds and coconut to the
flapjacks enhances both the flavour and
nutritional value of this easy recipe.

Bakewell tart; Flapjacks

SIMNEL CAKE

MAKES ABOUT 12–18 SLICES

175 g/6 oz soft vegetable margarine
150 g/5 oz muscovado sugar
3 free-range eggs
225 g/8 oz plain wholemeal flour
2½ teaspoons baking powder
50 g/2 oz ground almonds
¾ teaspoon cinnamon
100 g/4 oz raisins
100 g/4 oz sultanas
100 g/4 oz currants
50 g/2 oz split almonds, finely chopped
grated rind of 1 lemon
2 tablespoons skimmed milk
1 tablespoon no-sugar apricot jam
1 (227-g/8-oz) packet raw sugar marzipan
beaten egg white to glaze

Preparation time **30 minutes**
Cooking time **1¾–2 hours**
Oven temperature **160 C, 325 F, gas 3**

1 Cream together the margarine and sugar until light and fluffy. Beat in the eggs, one at a time. Sift in the flour, baking powder, the ground almonds and cinnamon and sprinkle in the bran remaining in the sieve. Add all the dried fruits, the chopped almonds and lemon rind and fold all the ingredients in with a metal spoon, adding milk to mix.

2 Pile the mixture into a greased and lined 20-cm/8-in round cake tin and press it down gently, smoothing the top. Bake the cake in the centre of the oven for 1¾–2 hours, until a skewer inserted in the centre comes out clean. Leave it to cool in the tin.

3 When quite cold, brush the top of the cake with apricot jam. Roll out the marzipan on a surface lightly dusted with icing sugar to a round 5 cm/2 in larger in diameter than the top of the cake. Place the round on the cake, trim off the surplus marzipan with a sharp knife and flute the edge.

4 Use the marzipan trimmings to make 11 small balls. Brush these with beaten egg white, place them on a baking tray and grill gently until golden brown. Place round the edge of the cake top.

Simnel cake

Whole recipe:

Calories 5,190

Fat 280g

Fibre 70g

WHOLEMEAL BREAD

MAKES 2 450-g/1-lb LOAVES OR 20 ROLLS

675 g/1½ lb plain wholemeal flour
½–1 teaspoon sea salt
25 g/1 oz vegetable margarine
25 g/1 oz fresh yeast
450 ml/¾ pint tepid water
1 (25-mg) vitamin C tablet, crushed
1 beaten free-range egg or skimmed milk to glaze
sesame, caraway or poppy seeds, cracked wheat or oatmeal for sprinkling (optional)

Preparation time **50 minutes**
Cooking time **20–40 minutes**
Oven temperature **230 C, 450 F, gas 8**

1 Mix the flour with the salt and rub in the margarine with your fingertips, lifting the mixture as you do so.

2 Crumble the yeast between your fingers into the warm water and add the crushed vitamin C tablet. Stir the mixture until thoroughly combined.

3 Pour the yeast liquid on to the flour and mix it in with your hands, drawing the dough together. Different flours have varying absorbencies, so add any extra water or flour gradually.

4 Turn the dough on to a lightly floured surface and knead it well. Knead the dough, folding it towards you and then pushing it away with the palm of the hand. Give it a quarter turn and continue, developing a rocking rhythm. Add a little extra flour if necessary, to prevent the dough becoming sticky; continue kneading for about 10 minutes until firm, smooth and elastic.

5 Cover the dough either with the upturned mixing bowl or with lightly greased polythene. Leave to rest for 10 minutes. Meanwhile, grease 2 450-g/ 1-lb loaf tins, or, if you are making rolls, two baking trays.

6 Divide the dough into two portions and shape them. Gently pull each portion into a rectangle three times the width of the tins. Fold into three and place in tins with the seam below.

7 Place the tins in a warm place and cover them with a damp towel or greased polythene. This stops a skin from forming on top of the dough. Leave the bread to prove until it has doubled in size and springs back when touched with the fingertips (30—40 minutes for loaves, 20—25 minutes for rolls). Do not overprove the dough as it can lose its elasticity and not rise fully.

8 Glaze the loaves with beaten egg or skimmed milk and sprinkle seeds, cracked wheat or oatmeal on top.

9 Bake loaves near the top of the oven for 30—40 minutes, rolls at the very top for 15—20 minutes until well-risen and golden brown. To test if the bread is ready; tip the loaves out of their tins and tap the bases; they should sound hollow. Cool on wire trays.

By adding a vitamin C tablet (ascorbic acid) to the dough, the time taken for the mixture to rise is much reduced. Decoratively shaped rolls can look particularly appetising.

Basic wholemeal bread

Whole loaf:
Calories 1,160
Fat 17g
Fibre 32g
Per roll:
Calories 115
Fat 2g
Fibre 3g

Simnel cake; Wholemeal bread and rolls

SUMMER

JUNE · JULY · AUGUST

Summer months abound with fresh, colourful foods from both home and abroad. Soft fruit is at its prime, as strawberries, raspberries, red and blackcurrants, apricots, peaches and cherries fill greengrocers' shelves. Later in August the first English plums and blackberries become available. Fresh vegetables are just as plentiful, with traditional salad ingredients at their best now. Lettuces, cucumbers, tomatoes, spring onions and radishes are excellent value as are peppers, aubergines and, later in the season, courgettes, both home-grown and imported from Mediterranean countries. French, runner and broad beans are at their best, as are peas, summer cauliflower and cabbages. Corn-on-the-cob and marrows begin to appear towards the end of August.

SUMMER MENUS

1

Flageolets Niçoise
Mushroom moussaka with green salad
Strawberry choux puffs

2

Cucumber soup with wholemeal croûtons
Avocado risotto with mange-tout and tofu stir-fry
Fresh fruit salad with natural yogurt

3

Tomato and thyme soup
Ratatouille with Greek salad
Fresh fruit

Black bean and mushroom soup

Per portion:

Calories 150

Fat 6g

Fibre 8g

BLACK BEAN AND MUSHROOM SOUP

SERVES 4

100 g/4 oz black kidney beans, soaked overnight
½ tablespoon sunflower oil
100 g/4 oz onion, finely chopped
1½ tablespoons plain wholemeal flour
1.5 litres/2¾ pints cold water
225 g/8 oz flat mushrooms, finely diced
1 teaspoon Vecon
1 tablespoon tomato purée
1 bay leaf
pinch of stoneground mustard
freshly ground pepper
chopped parsley to garnish

Preparation time **10 minutes plus overnight soaking**
Cooking time **1½ hours**

1 Drain the beans and set aside.
2 Heat the oil in a large saucepan and cook the onion for 1 minute. Stir in the flour and cook for another minute. Gradually add the water, stirring in well.
3 Add the mushrooms, kidney beans, Vecon, tomato purée, bay leaf and mustard. Bring to the boil, lower and simmer for 1–1¼ hours or until the beans are tender. Top up with extra water, if necessary.
4 Season with black pepper to taste and serve garnished with parsley.

An unusual soup; serve with wholemeal bread for a balanced protein intake. Ideal for lunchtime snacks.

Corn chowder	
Per portion:	
Calories 400	
Fat 4g	
Fibre 5g	

Black bean and mushroom soup; Corn chowder

CORN CHOWDER

SERVES 4

*1 tablespoon sunflower oil
100 g/4 oz onion, finely chopped
½ celery stick, finely chopped
225 g/8 oz potatoes, scrubbed and diced
225 g/8 oz sweetcorn kernels
600 ml/1 pint skimmed milk
200 ml/7 fl oz cold water
¼ teaspoon of Vecon*
½ teaspoon dried thyme
¼ teaspoon dried sage
1 green pepper, deseeded and finely chopped or 100 g/4 oz courgettes, finely chopped
freshly ground black pepper*

*Vegetable stock concentrate available from health food shops

Preparation time **10 minutes**
Cooking time **30 minutes**

1 Heat the oil in a saucepan and add the onions, celery and potatoes, cook together for 2 minutes, softening but not browning the vegetables.
2 Stir in the sweetcorn kernels, milk, water, Vecon, thyme and sage. Bring to the boil, cover, reduce heat and simmer very gently for 20 minutes.
3 Stir in the pepper or courgettes and cook for a further 5 minutes. Season with black pepper to taste and serve.

A substantial soup, popular with children for its creamy texture. It is ideal for those chilly winter lunchtimes.

Microwave note

Place the oil, onion, celery and garlic in a large heatproof dish and cook on full power for 3 minutes. Stir in the remaining ingredients and cook for a further 15 minutes, stirring once.

Tomato and thyme soup

Per portion:
Calories 60
Fat 4g
Fibre 2g

Freezing note

Like most soups, this soup freezes well, in a rigid airtight container or heavy duty polythene bag. Thaw at room temperature rather than in the microwave as the soup is to be served cold.

TOMATO AND THYME SOUP

SERVES 4

1 tablespoon olive oil
100 g/4 oz onion, chopped
½ celery stick, chopped
1 clove garlic, crushed
450 g/1 lb tomatoes, peeled and chopped
1 red pepper, deseeded and chopped
450 ml/¾ pint vegetable stock
½ teaspoon chopped fresh thyme
1 bay leaf
freshly ground black pepper

*Preparation time **20 minutes***
*Cooking time **35 minutes***

1 Heat the oil and cook the onion, celery and garlic over a low heat for 2 minutes. **2** Add the tomatoes, pepper, stock, thyme and bay leaf. Bring to the boil, cover and reduce heat. Simmer for 30 minutes. Remove bay leaf, season with pepper and serve.

This is a light, low-calorie, refreshing soup. A good lunch dish or starter. Serve with either fresh wholemeal bread or wholemeal croûtons.

Variations
This soup can be varied by omitting the red pepper and using 100 g/4 oz finely grated carrot in its place. Alternatively, a green or yellow pepper could be used instead of the red pepper to give a more colourful effect.

Tomato and thyme soup;
Cucumber soup

CUCUMBER SOUP

SERVES 4

100g/4oz onion, chopped
100g/4oz potato, peeled and chopped
1 tablespoon sunflower oil
275g/10oz cucumber, peeled and diced
300ml/½ pint skimmed milk
300ml/½ pint vegetable stock
1 bay leaf
250ml/8fl oz natural yogurt
freshly ground black pepper
freshly chopped chives to garnish

Preparation time **15–20 minutes**
Cooking time **25 minutes**

1 Cook the onion and potato in the oil for 2 minutes. Add the cucumber and cook for 1 minute. Add the milk, stock and bay leaf. Bring to the boil, reduce heat and simmer for 20 minutes until the vegetables are quite soft.
2 Discard the bay leaf and blend the soup in a liquidiser. Stir in the yogurt, reserving 2 tablespoons. Leave to cool and season to taste with pepper. Divide between four serving bowls and garnish with the remaining yogurt and chives.

Low in calories, this refreshing summer soup looks pretty when served garnished with a swirl of natural yogurt and chives.

Variations
Courgettes could be used in place of the cucumber. Use the same weight (275g/ 10oz) and proceed as detailed, adding a sprig of fresh tarragon (or ½ teaspoon dried) to the mixture with the bay leaf. Leave out the potato and cucumber and use instead two avocados, peeled and chopped.

Cucumber soup	
Per portion:	
Calories 100	
Fat 4g	
Fibre 2g	

CANNELLINI AND ALMOND SOUP

SERVES 4

100 g/4 oz cannellini beans, soaked overnight
8 tablespoons olive oil
2 cloves garlic, crushed
1 leek or 100 g/4 oz onions, finely chopped
900 ml/1½ pints vegetable stock
175 ml/6 fl oz dry white wine
75 g/3 oz ground almonds
freshly ground black pepper
2 tablespoons flaked almonds, toasted

*Preparation time **10 minutes plus overnight soaking and 4 hours to chill***
*Cooking time **80 minutes***

1 Drain the beans and set aside.
2 Heat the oil in a saucepan and cook the garlic and leek over a low heat for 2 minutes. Add the drained beans, stock and wine. Bring to the boil, cover and reduce heat to a simmer. Cook for 30 minutes.
3 Stir in the ground almonds and cook for a further 45 minutes or until the beans are soft. Blend the soup in a liquidiser to a smooth púree and chill for 4 hours.
4 Take out of the refrigerator 15 minutes before serving. Season with black pepper and serve garnished with the flaked almonds.

This is a delicious creamy soup which is high in fibre.

Cannellini and almond soup

Per portion:	
Calories	280
Fat	18g
Fibre	10g

GAZPACHO

SERVES 4

*450 g/ 1 lb ripe tomatoes, peeled,
deseeded and chopped
1 large cucumber, peeled and diced
225 g/8 oz onion, diced
1 large green pepper, deseeded and
diced
3 cloves garlic, peeled
1 tablespoon white wine vinegar
4 tablespoons olive oil
600 ml/ 1 pint cold water*
Garnish
*1 small red pepper, deseeded and
diced
4 tomatoes, roughly chopped
¼ cucumber, diced*

Preparation time **30 minutes plus
time to chill**

1 Place the chopped tomatoes, cucumber, onion and pepper in a large serving dish.
2 In a small bowl crush the garlic, stir in the vinegar and gradually add the oil to make a smooth paste. Stir this into the vegetable mixture and add the water. Stir together well and chill.
3 Serve the soup with the vegetable garnishes in small bowls separately.

For summer days, chilled soups are perfect. This is a traditional Spanish soup, refreshing to eat and low in calories.

Gazpacho

Per portion:

Calories 180

Fat 15g

Fibre 3g

Cannellini and almond soup; Gazpacho

Spinach and avocado salad

Per portion:

Calories 440

Fat 40g

Fibre 10g

Potato salad with garlic

Per portion:

Calories 190

Fat 6g

Fibre 4g

SPINACH AND AVOCADO SALAD

S E R V E S 4

450g/1 lb young spinach leaves
3 tablespoons olive oil
1 clove garlic, crushed
1 tablespoon fresh lemon juice
freshly ground black pepper
50g/2oz sunflower seeds
2 ripe avocados

*Preparation time **15 minutes***
*Cooking time **2–3 minutes***

1 Gently tear the spinach leaves away from the stalks and tear into small shreds. Place in a bowl.
2 In a screw-topped jar shake together the oil, garlic and lemon juice with a dash of freshly ground black pepper. Pour over the spinach and toss thoroughly.
3 Lightly toast the sunflower seeds for 2–3 minutes either under a very hot grill or in a heavy-based frying pan. Set aside.
4 Cut the avocados in half and remove the stones. Cut the flesh away from the skin and slice thinly. Arrange on top of the spinach in the bowl. Toss the sunflower seeds on top, and serve at once.

Spinach and avocado salad

The mixture of spinach and avocado is delightful. Make sure the avocados are quite ripe and the spinach tender.

Variation
Fresh spinach is not always easy to come by in shops so a colourful alternative is to use peeled segments of three large oranges with the sliced avocado instead of the spinach in this recipe. Omit the olive oil and simply shake the garlic with 2 tablespoons lemon juice and scatter over the orange segments, then top with the toasted sunflower seeds.

POTATO SALAD WITH GARLIC

S E R V E S 4

675g/1½ lb new potatoes, scrubbed
sprig fresh mint
2 tablespoons mayonnaise
2 tablespoons natural yogurt
2 cloves garlic, crushed
¼ cucumber, finely diced
2 mint leaves, chopped
freshly ground black pepper

*Preparation time **15 minutes***
*Cooking time **25 minutes plus 1 hour to chill***

1 Place the potatoes in a pan of cold water, to just cover. Add the mint. Bring to the boil then simmer for 15–20 minutes until cooked. Drain and remove the mint.
2 Immediately beat the mayonnaise with the yogurt and crushed garlic and toss the potatoes in this dressing.
3 Stir in the cucumber and mint leaves and season to taste with black pepper. Leave to chill for 1 hour before serving.

Using some yogurt in place of mayonnaise helps to keep the fat content of this tasty salad down.

Potato salad with garlic

Mediterranean shells;
Mushrooms à la Grecque

MEDITERRANEAN SHELLS

SERVES 4

75 g/3 oz wholewheat pasta shells
1 tablespoon olive oil
75 g/3 oz onion, finely chopped
1 clove garlic
350 g/12 oz fresh tomatoes, peeled and chopped
175 g/6 oz courgettes, cut into 2.5-cm/ 1-in long matchsticks
2 tablespoons basil
freshly ground black pepper

Preparation time **10 minutes**
Cooking time **30 minutes**

1 Place the pasta shells in a saucepan of boiling water to cook. Cook for 10–12 minutes until *al dente*, almost tender. Drain and set aside while preparing the sauce.
2 Heat the oil in a saucepan, add the onion and garlic and cook for 2 minutes. Add the tomatoes and cook for another 8 minutes.
3 Stir in the courgettes and cook for a further 4 minutes.
4 Add the basil, season with black pepper and then stir in the pasta shells. Cook for 2 minutes, then serve in individual dishes. Hot garlic bread is an excellent accompaniment.

This light, colourful starter makes good use of courgettes and tomatoes, both plentiful in the summer months. Wholewheat pasta shells supply more fibre and vital vitamins and minerals than white pasta. Try not to overcook the pasta; it should still have a little 'bite' left in it.

MUSHROOMS À LA GRECQUE

SERVES 4

4 cloves garlic, crushed
4 ripe tomatoes, peeled and chopped
3 tablespoons olive oil
2 tablespoons dry cider
2 tablespoons tomato purée
250 ml/8 fl oz cold water
8 coriander seeds
1 bay leaf
sprig of thyme or $\frac{1}{4}$ teaspoon dried thyme
$\frac{1}{4}$ teaspoon oregano
450 g/1 lb button mushrooms

Preparation time **10 minutes plus 1 hour to chill**
Cooking time **25 minutes**

1 Place the garlic and tomatoes in a saucepan with the remaining ingredients, except the mushrooms. Bring to the boil, cover and cook gently for 10 minutes.
2 Add the mushrooms to the pan and cook for another 6 minutes until they are just soft but not soggy.
3 Remove the mushrooms from the pan and arrange in 4 serving dishes.
4 Cook the sauce over a fierce heat for 5–7 minutes, uncovered to reduce it. Sieve, then pour over the mushrooms. Chill for 1 hour and serve.

This tasty low-calorie starter can also be made with other vegetables in place of the mushrooms – courgettes and cauliflower florets are both ideal.

Microwave note
This dish can be easily made in advance and then reheated in the microwave on full power for 4 minutes.

Mediterranean shells

Per portion:
Calories 125
Fat 4g
Fibre 4g

Mushrooms à la Grecque

Per portion:
Calories 130
Fat 11g
Fibre 4g

FLAGEOLETS NIÇOISE

SERVES 4

225 g/8 oz flageolet beans, soaked
1 clove garlic, peeled
4 large ripe tomatoes
1 large red pepper
12 black olives
2 tablespoons olive oil
1 tablespoon white wine vinegar
1 tablespoon chopped parsley
1 tablespoon chopped chives
2 hard-boiled, free-range eggs, chopped
freshly ground black pepper

Preparation time **20 minutes, plus overnight soaking**
Cooking time **1¼ hours**

1 Drain the beans, place in saucepan of cold water and cook for 1–1¼ hours or until tender. Drain.

2 Rub the garlic clove around the inside of the bowl you will be serving the salad in. Chop the tomatoes. Deseed and chop the pepper and stone the olives.

3 Place the oil and vinegar with the parsley and chives in a clean screw-topped jar. As soon as the beans are cooked, shake the dressing ingredients together and pour over the beans. Stir in the egg, tomatoes, pepper and olives and place in the salad bowl. Season with pepper and serve when the beans have cooled.

More expensive than other dried beans the flageolet bean should be reserved for special dishes, like this attractive and flavourful salad; perfect for warm summer days, served as a light first course, or as an accompaniment.

Flageolets Niçoise

Per portion:
Calories 300
Fat 13g
Fibre 13g

Flageolets Niçoise

MUSHROOM MOUSSAKA

SERVES 4

450 g / 1 lb aubergine
sea salt
150 ml / $\frac{1}{4}$ pint tomato juice
1 tablespoon olive oil
100 g / 4 oz onion, chopped
2 cloves garlic, crushed
350 g / 12 oz button mushrooms, sliced
1 red pepper, deseeded and chopped
450 g / 1 lb tomatoes, peeled and chopped
$\frac{1}{2}$ teaspoon dried or 1 teaspoon chopped fresh marjoram
1 bay leaf
3 free-range eggs
300 ml / $\frac{1}{2}$ pint natural yogurt
freshly ground black pepper
50 g / 2 oz farmhouse Cheddar cheese, finely grated

Preparation time **45 minutes**
Cooking time **75 minutes**
Oven temperature **190 C, 375 F, gas 5**

1 Cut the aubergine into 5-mm/$\frac{1}{4}$-in thick slices, sprinkle with sea salt and leave to stand for 30 minutes. Rinse and wipe dry.

(This process removes some of the bitterness of the aubergine.)
2 Poach the aubergine slices in the tomato juice for 3 minutes each side. Set aside.
3 Heat the oil in a separate pan and cook the onion and garlic gently for 2 minutes. Stir in the mushrooms, pepper and tomatoes and any extra juice remaining from the pan used to poach the aubergine. If using dried marjoram add to the pan with a bay leaf. Bring to the boil, then reduce heat and simmer for 20 minutes. If using fresh marjoram, add at this stage.
4 Place a layer of aubergine in a lightly oiled ovenproof dish, top with a layer of sauce, add remaining aubergines and finish with the remaining sauce. In a jug beat together the eggs and yogurt with pepper and pour on top.
5 Sprinkle with the grated cheese and bake for 30–40 minutes. Serve at once.

A rich vegetable and mushroom sauce replaces the lamb usually used in this traditional Greek dish. To cut down on fat, the aubergine is cooked in tomato juice rather than oil.

Microwave note
The entire dish could be prepared in the microwave to save time. Poach the aubergine slices on full power for 2 minutes each side. Heat the onion and garlic in the oil on full power for 2 minutes, add the tomatoes, mushrooms, herbs and pepper and cook on full power for 8 minutes. Layer the aubergine with sauce, top with the egg and yogurt mixture and cook on full power for 5 minutes. Add the cheese and cook for a further minute to melt the cheese.

Mushroom moussaka
Per portion:
Calories 250
Fat 13g
Fibre 7g

Microwave note
The sauce could be made in advance, but do not add the avocado until just before serving. Reheat in the microwave on full power for 3 minutes, stir and heat for a further 3 minutes. Proceed as recipe from stage 3.

Avocado risotto

Per portion:

Calories **480**

Fat **18g**

Fibre **7g**

Courgette soufflé quiche

Per portion:

Calories **330**

Fat **21g**

Fibre **4g**

AVOCADO RISOTTO

SERVES 4

100 g/4 oz onion, chopped
2 cloves garlic, crushed
I tablespoon olive oil
450 g/1 lb tomatoes, peeled and chopped
225 g/8 oz mushrooms, halved
150 ml/¼ pint dry white wine
I teaspoon chopped fresh or ½ teaspoon dried basil
275 g/10 oz long-grain brown rice
I large or 2 small avocados
freshly ground black pepper
freshly grated Parmesan cheese to serve

Preparation time **10 minutes**
Cooking time **30 minutes**

1 Cook the onion and garlic in the oil over a low heat for 2 minutes. Add the tomatoes, mushrooms, wine and dried basil, if using. Bring to the boil, reduce the heat and simmer for 20 minutes.
2 Meanwhile place the rice in a pan with enough cold water to cover. Bring to the boil, then reduce to a steady simmer and cook for 25 minutes or until the rice is tender.
3 Cut the avocado(s) in half and remove the stone(s). Slice the flesh and add to the sauce with the fresh basil, if using, and freshly ground black pepper to taste. Heat through while the rice nears the end of its cooking time.
4 Drain the rice and arrange on the serving plates. Pour the sauce into the centre of the rice and serve at once, with freshly grated Parmesan.

Avocados are rarely served hot, but this special risotto includes warm avocado. For the special effect in the picture, cook an additional 175 g/6 oz rice, place in a 20-cm/8-in ring tin and bake for 5 minutes in a moderately hot oven (200 C, 400 F, gas 6) before turning out and serving the sauce in the centre.

COURGETTE SOUFFLÉ QUICHE

SERVES 4

Pastry
100 g/4 oz plain wholemeal flour
50 g/2 oz soft vegetable margarine
cold water to mix
Filling
175 g/6 oz courgettes, chopped
20 g/¾ oz soft vegetable margarine
20 g/¾ oz plain wholemeal flour
150 ml/¼ pint skimmed milk
freshly ground black pepper
40 g/1½ oz farmhouse Cheddar cheese, finely grated
2 free-range eggs

Preparation time **35 minutes, plus 20 minutes to chill**
Cooking time **35 minutes**
Oven temperature **200 C, 400 F, gas 6**

1 Sift the flour into a mixing bowl, adding the bran from the sieve. Rub in the margarine until the mixture resembles fine breadcrumbs. Chill for 20 minutes. Add just sufficient cold water to mix to a soft dough. Roll out on a lightly floured surface to a circle just larger than an 18-cm/7-in flan dish or ring, line and bake blind for 10 minutes.
2 Steam or cook the courgettes in a little boiling water for 5 minutes. Drain.
3 Melt the margarine in a saucepan and stir in the flour. Cook for 1 minute, then gradually add the milk, beating constantly. Bring to the boil to let the sauce thicken. Season and stir in the Cheddar.
4 Separate the eggs and beat the egg yolks into the sauce. Add the courgettes. Whisk the egg whites until they stand in stiff peaks and using a metal tablespoon, fold a little of the mixture into the sauce, then carefully fold in the remainder. Pour into the baked pastry case and bake for 20 minutes until the mixture is just firm to the touch and golden brown.

Serve this impressive quiche as soon as it is cooked, before it collapses.

Microwave note
**Bake the pastry case
blind in the microwave
on full power for 4
minutes. Remove the
paper and continue to
cook for 1 minute. The
sauce can also be
prepared in the
microwave. Melt the
margarine on full
power for 1 minute.
Add the flour and cook
for 1 minute. Heat the
milk on full power for
2 minutes, then stir
into the flour roux.
Return to the
microwave for a
further 2 minutes to
cook. Season and stir in
the Cheddar. Proceed
from stage 4 of
Courgette soufflé quiche.**

*Avocado risotto;
Courgette soufflé
quiche*

Microwave note
The dish can be prepared in 20 minutes in the microwave, but I find the flavours develop better by cooking on the hob for a longer period of time. It is, however, useful to start the dish off in the microwave. Heat the oil, onion and garlic on full power for 2 minutes. Stir in the diced aubergines, return to the microwave for a further 2 minutes. Then transfer to a saucepan and proceed, adding the remaining ingredients.

Freezing note
Freeze in rigid containers. Defrost at room temperature or on defrost setting in the microwave for 15 minutes plus 5 minutes standing time.

Ratatouille	
Per portion:	
Calories 100	
Fat 8g	
Fibre 3g	

Ratatouille

RATATOUILLE

SERVES 4

225 g/8 oz aubergine
2 tablespoons olive oil
100 g/4 oz onion, chopped
2 cloves garlic, crushed
225 g/8 oz courgettes, sliced
1 green pepper, deseeded and sliced
1 red pepper, deseeded and sliced
450 g/1 lb tomatoes, peeled and chopped
½ teaspoon dried or 2 teaspoons fresh chopped basil

Preparation time **15 minutes**
Cooking time **50 minutes**

1 Cut the aubergine into 1-cm/½-in cubes.
2 Heat the oil in a large saucepan. Add the onion and garlic and cook for 2 minutes

without browning. Add the aubergine and cook for a further 2 minutes. Add the dried basil, if using, and remaining ingredients, slowly bring to the boil, cover with a tight-fitting lid, reduce the heat and simmer for 45 minutes. Add the fresh basil 5 minutes before the end of cooking. Season with pepper. Serve hot or chilled.

When Mediterranean vegetables are so cheap in the summer months, make batches of ratatouille and freeze for use on dull winter days. Fresh basil gives the best flavour, but dried can be used in its place. Add dried basil with the tomatoes to let the flavour develop; fresh basil should be added near the end of cooking.

Ratatouille

*Mange-tout and tofu
stir-fry*

MANGE-TOUT AND TOFU STIR-FRY

SERVES 4

*450 g / 1 lb tofu
225 g / 8 oz mange-tout peas
2 spring onions
1 tablespoon sesame oil
1 clove garlic, crushed
2 tablespoons vegetable stock
2 teaspoons soy sauce
2 teaspoons dry sherry or rice wine*

*Preparation time **20 minutes**
Cooking time **5 minutes***

1 Squeeze out gently any excess moisture from the tofu in a clean tea-towel. Unwrap and cut into 1-cm/½-in cubes.

2 Wash the mange-tout peas and trim any stalks. Trim away the roots and coarse leaves from the spring onions, cut in half and then slice lengthwise into four.

3 Heat the oil in a wok or large frying pan. Add the garlic and heat for 2 minutes. Add the mange-tout peas and tofu and coat in the oil. Heat for 1 minute. Add the stock, soy sauce and sherry or rice wine and cook for a further 2 minutes, stirring well. Add the spring onions, stir in and serve at once.

Tofu is a versatile low-calorie, low-fat food which is made from soya beans. Lacking in any distinct flavour of its own, tofu lends itself to a whole variety of both savoury and sweet dishes.

**Mange-tout and tofu
stir-fry**

Per portion:
Calories 150
Fat 8g
Fibre 2g

PIZZA PIECES

MAKES 10 PIECES

Dough

225 g/8 oz plain wholemeal flour
¼ teaspoon sea salt
¼ teaspoon chopped fresh or dried basil
15 g/½ oz fresh yeast
1 (25-mg) vitamin C tablet
150 ml/¼ pint lukewarm water
1 tablespoon olive oil

Topping

1 clove garlic, crushed
75 g/3 oz onion, finely chopped
100 g/4 oz carrot, finely diced
1 red pepper, deseeded and finely chopped
1 tablespoon olive oil
450 g/1 lb tomatoes, peeled and chopped
1 tablespoon tomato purée
½ teaspoon chopped fresh or dried basil
225 g/8 oz sweetcorn kernels
100 g/4 oz mushrooms, finely chopped
175–225 g/6–8 oz mozzarella cheese, thinly sliced
2 tablespoons grated Parmesan cheese
freshly ground black pepper

Preparation time **30–35 minutes**
Cooking time **12–15 minutes**
Oven temperature **240 C, 475 F, gas 9**

---

1 First prepare a tomato sauce for the topping. Place the garlic, onion, carrot and half the chopped red pepper into a saucepan with the oil and cook gently over a low heat for 3 minutes.
2 Stir in the chopped tomatoes, tomato purée and basil and bring to the boil. Cover, reduce the heat and simmer for 30 minutes, or until thickened.
3 Heat the oven to 240 C, 475 F, gas 9 and lightly oil a baking tray. For the dough, place the flour in a large mixing bowl with the salt and basil. Crumble the yeast and the vitamin C tablet into the water and stir until dissolved. Stir in the olive oil and add to flour mixture.
4 Using your hands mix the ingredients together to form a smooth dough. Turn the dough out on to a lightly floured surface and knead for 5 minutes. Cover

and leave to rest for 5 minutes.
5 Roll out the dough into a rectangle measuring 20 × 25 cm/8 × 10 in. Place on the prepared baking tray. Spread the tomato sauce over the dough, leaving a good 5 mm/¼ in space all round the edge. Sprinkle the sweetcorn, remaining red pepper and mushrooms over the pizza and arrange the mozzarella cheese on top. Sprinkle the Parmesan over and season with pepper.
6 Bake immediately at the top of the heated oven, for 12–15 minutes or until the dough is well risen and slightly browned round the edges. The cheese should be melted, bubbling and golden. Cut into ten pieces and serve at once.

PINE KERNEL PIZZAS

MAKES 8

Sauce

1 teaspoon olive oil
1 small onion, finely chopped
1 clove garlic, crushed
1 (425-g/15-oz) can or 450 g/1 lb fresh tomatoes, peeled
1 red pepper, deseeded and chopped
1 teaspoon basil or oregano

Dough

225 g/8 oz plain wholemeal flour
15 g/½ oz soft vegetable margarine
pinch of sea salt
15 g/½ oz fresh yeast
1 (25-mg) vitamin C tablet
150 ml/¼ pint tepid water

Topping

50 g/2 oz pine kernels
50 g/2 oz mushrooms, sliced
1 green pepper, deseeded and chopped
175 g/6 oz mozzarella or Edam cheese, cut into fine strips
4 olives, halved and stoned

Preparation time **50 minutes plus 20 minutes to rise**
Cooking time **55 minutes**
Oven temperature **220 C, 425 F, gas 7**

---

1 To make the tomato sauce. Heat the oil in a saucepan, add the onion and garlic together and cook over a low heat

---

Pizza pieces

Per portion:

Calories 210

Fat 9g

Fibre 5g

Pine kernel pizzas

Per pizza:

Calories 230

Fat 12g

Fibre 4g

Pizza pieces; Pine kernel pizzas

for 2 minutes. Add the tomatoes, peeled if using fresh, pepper and herbs. Bring to the boil, cover, reduce heat and simmer for 30 minutes.

2 Meanwhile make the dough. Place the flour in a bowl, rub in the margarine and stir in salt. Place the yeast and vitamin C in a bowl, add the tepid water and stir. Pour onto flour and mix to a dough.

3 Turn out on a lightly floured surface and knead for 6 minutes until smooth.

Cover and leave to rest for 10 minutes.

4 The dough is now ready to use. Roll out to 5-mm/¼-in thick. Cut out 8, 7.5-cm/3-in rounds and place on lightly greased baking trays. Spoon the sauce on top and add topping ingredients, finishing with the cheese and topping each pizza with an olive half.

5 Leave in a warm place to rise for 20 minutes, then bake at the top of the oven for 15–20 minutes. Serve hot.

Microwave note

The microwave cooks scrambled eggs quickly. The entire dish can be prepared on full power. Heat the onion, garlic and butter or oil for 2 minutes. Add the pepper, tomatoes and cook for 2 minutes. Add the eggs and cook for 2 minutes. Stir well and cook for a further 3 minutes or until set.

*Stuffed peppers;
Pipérade*

Pipérade	
Per portion:	
Calories 180	
Fat 13g	
Fibre 1g	

PIPÉRADE

SERVES 4

*25g/1oz butter or 1 tablespoon olive oil
50g/2oz onion, chopped
1 clove garlic, crushed
1 green pepper, deseeded and chopped
6 free-range eggs, beaten
freshly ground black pepper
225g/8oz tomatoes, peeled and chopped
pinch of chilli powder
chopped parsley to garnish*

*Preparation time **10 minutes**
Cooking time **7 minutes***

1 Heat the butter or oil in a saucepan and cook the onion, garlic and pepper for 2 minutes.
2 Season the eggs with pepper, stir into the pan and cook over a low heat, stirring constantly, for 3 minutes.
3 Add the tomatoes and chilli powder, and cook for a further 2 minutes or until the eggs are set. Serve at once, garnished with chopped parsley.

This Mediterranean dish transforms scrambled egg into a nutritious lunch.

STUFFED PEPPERS

SERVES 4

100 g/4 oz haricot beans, soaked overnight
100 g/4 oz onion, chopped
2 cloves garlic, crushed
1 tablespoon olive oil
450 g/1 lb fresh tomatoes, peeled and chopped
100 g/4 oz mushrooms, sliced
½ teaspoon dried or 1 teaspoon chopped fresh basil
4 red or green medium peppers
75 g/3 oz farmhouse Cheddar cheese, grated
3 tablespoons sunflower seeds

Preparation time **10 minutes, plus overnight soaking**
Cooking time **2 hours 10 minutes**

1 Drain the beans and cook for 1–1½ hours in a pan of water until soft; alternatively pressure cook for 10 minutes at 6.75-kg/15-lb pressure. Drain.

2 Cook the onion and garlic in the oil for 2 minutes. Stir in the tomatoes, mushrooms and dried basil, if using, and bring to the boil. Reduce the heat and simmer for 20 minutes; add fresh basil at this stage, if using. Stir in the beans and simmer for a further 5 minutes.

3 Cut the peppers in half lengthwise, deseed and blanch in a pan of boiling water for 2 minutes. Drain thoroughly and arrange in a shallow flameproof dish. Fill each half with the sauce. Scatter the cheese on top of the peppers with the sunflower seeds. Place under a hot grill for 4–5 minutes until the topping is golden and bubbling. Serve at once.

This unusual filling combines haricot beans with the best of summer's fresh produce in a nutritious supper dish. Serve with wholemeal pasta.

Microwave note
The sauce can be prepared using the microwave. At stage 2, place the onion, garlic and oil in a covered casserole dish on full power and cook for 2 minutes. Add the tomatoes, mushrooms and dried basil and cook for a further 5 minutes. Add the beans and fresh basil and cook for a further 2 minutes. Then place the blanched peppers, filled and topped with cheese and sunflower seeds in the microwave on full power for 3 minutes. Serve at once.

Stuffed peppers	
Per portion:	
Calories 280	
Fat 15g	
Fibre 10g	

Tomato and soft cheese quiche

Per portion:

Calories 250

Fat 14g

Fibre 4g

Microwave note

Both these quiches could be prepared using the microwave to cook the pastry cases blind for 4 minutes. The filling for the Provençal tart could be prepared in the microwave by heating the onion, garlic and oil together on full power for 4 minutes. Add the tomatoes, pepper, tomato purée and basil, and cook for a further 10 minutes. Pour into the prepared flan case, garnish with olives and cook on full power for another 4 minutes.

Provençal tart

Per portion:

Calories 240

Fat 15g

Fibre 4g

TOMATO AND SOFT CHEESE QUICHE

SERVES 4

Pastry
100g/4oz plain wholemeal flour
50g/2oz soft vegetable margarine
cold water to mix
Filling
275g/10oz tomatoes
3 spring onions, finely chopped
2 free-range eggs
100g/4oz low-fat soft cheese
1 tablespoon tomato purée
½ teaspoon basil or marjoram
freshly ground black pepper

Preparation time **25 minutes plus 15 minutes to chill**
Cooking time **30 minutes**
Oven temperature **200C, 400F, gas 6**
190C, 375F, gas 5

1 Place the flour in a bowl and rub in the margarine until the mixture resembles fine breadcrumbs. Place in the refrigerator to chill for 10–15 minutes.
2 Meanwhile, prepare the filling. Peel the tomatoes by plunging into a bowl of boiling water; stand for one minute, then remove and peel away the skin and chop finely. Add the spring onions and mix well.
3 Beat the eggs with soft cheese and add the tomato purée, basil and some black pepper to season. Pour onto the tomato and onion mixture.
4 When the pastry mixture has chilled, add just enough water to mix to a soft dough and then roll out on a lightly floured board. Line an 18-cm/7-in flan dish or ring with greaseproof paper, add the pastry and bake blind for 10 minutes.
5 Pour filling into the baked pastry case, reduce the heat and bake for 20 minutes until set.

A deliciously light quiche which can be served either hot or cold with a salad.

PROVENCAL TART

SERVES 4

Pastry
100g/4oz plain wholemeal flour
50g/2oz soft vegetable margarine
cold water to mix
Filling
1 tablespoon olive oil
225g/8oz onion, finely sliced
1 clove garlic, crushed
350g/12oz tomatoes, peeled and chopped
1 small green pepper, deseeded and chopped
2 tablespoons tomato purée
½ teaspoon basil
8 black olives

Preparation time **15 minutes plus 10 minutes to chill**
Cooking time **35 minutes**
Oven temperature **190C, 375F, gas 5**

1 Place the flour in a bowl and rub in the margarine until the mixture resembles fine breadcrumbs. Chill for 10 minutes. Add just enough cold water to the pastry mixture to make a soft dough, roll out and line a greased 18-cm/7-in flan dish or ring. Alternatively, cook the tart in an oblong flan dish. Bake blind for 10 minutes.
2 Meanwhile, prepare the filling. Heat the oil in a saucepan and cook the onion and garlic for 2 minutes over a low heat.
3 Add the tomatoes, pepper, tomato purée and basil. Bring to the boil, cover, reduce heat and cook for 10 minutes.
4 Pour the filling into the baked flan case, arrange the olives on top and bake for 20 minutes or until the filling is set. Serve hot or cold.

A richly coloured dish, suitable for vegans as it is free from dairy produce.

Provençal tart; Tomato and soft cheese quiche

Microwave note

To prepare New potatoes with tomatoes and mushrooms in the microwave. First cook the potatoes: put them in a microwaveproof serving dish, add 2 tablespoons water and cover. Cook on full power for 10–12 minutes or until tender, rearranging the vegetables halfway through cooking. Set aside.

For the sauce, put the onion, garlic and oil in a basin, then cover and cook on full power for 2 minutes. Stir in the tomatoes and cook on full power for a further 1 minute. Stir in the mushrooms, pepper and basil and cover. Cook on full power for 10 minutes, stir and cook for a final 5 minutes. Season to taste.

Drain any cooking liquid from the potatoes, pour over the sauce and finish as in the main recipe.

New potatoes with tomatoes and mushrooms

Per portion:

Calories 320

Fat 9g

Fibre 10g

New potatoes with almonds and herbs

Per portion:

Calories 370

Fat 16g

Fibre 7g

NEW POTATOES WITH ALMONDS AND HERBS

S E R V E S 4

1 kg/2 lb small new potatoes, scrubbed
25 g/1 oz butter or 2 tablespoons olive oil
1 clove garlic, crushed (optional)
50 g/2 oz flaked almonds
4 spring onions, chopped
1 tablespoon chopped fresh or 2 teaspoons dried marjoram
1 teaspoon chopped fresh mint
freshly ground black pepper
150 ml/$\frac{1}{4}$ pint strained, Greek-style yogurt
sprigs of mint to garnish

Preparation time **15 minutes**
Cooking time **20–25 minutes**

1 Cook the potatoes in boiling water until tender – about 15 minutes, then drain.
2 Melt the butter or heat the oil in a pan and add the garlic (if using) with the almonds. Cook, stirring frequently, over a medium heat until the nuts are lightly browned.
3 Add the potatoes, spring onions and herbs to the pan. Stir well to combine the ingredients and cook for a minute.
4 Transfer the potatoes to a warmed serving dish, swirl yogurt around them and garnish with sprigs of mint. Serve immediately.

NEW POTATOES WITH TOMATOES AND MUSHROOMS

S E R V E S 4

175 g/6 oz onion, finely chopped
2 cloves garlic, crushed
2 tablespoons olive oil
450 g/1 lb tomatoes, peeled and chopped
450 g/1 lb open flat mushrooms, sliced
1 red pepper, deseeded and sliced
1 teaspoon dried or 2 teaspoons chopped fresh basil
1 kg/2 lb small new potatoes, scrubbed
freshly ground black pepper
2 tablespoons grated Parmesan cheese
chopped fresh basil or parsley to garnish

Preparation time **20 minutes**
Cooking time **50 minutes**

1 Cook the onion and garlic in the olive oil, over a low heat without browning.
2 Add the tomatoes to the pan and cook for a minute, then stir in the mushrooms and pepper. Bring to the boil, then add the dried basil if using (add fresh basil 5 minutes before the end of the cooking time). Cover and simmer for 40 minutes, stirring occasionally to prevent the mixture from sticking. Add a little extra water if necessary during cooking.
3 Ten minutes before the sauce is ready cook the potatoes in boiling water until just tender.
4 Drain the potatoes and put them in a serving dish. Season the sauce, pour it over the potatoes and mix lightly, then sprinkle with the Parmesan cheese. Serve immediately, garnished with the chopped basil or parsley.

New potatoes with
tomatoes and
mushrooms; New
potatoes with almonds
and herbs

PESTO

SERVES 4

12 basil sprigs
1 clove garlic
4 tablespoons grated Parmesan cheese
1 tablespoon pine nuts
4–5 tablespoons olive oil

Preparation time **25 minutes**

1 Wash the basil, pat dry and strip the leaves from the stems. Place the leaves in a pestle and mortar with the garlic and crush together until smooth.
2 Gradually add the cheese and pine nuts, working up a paste, with the oil. The texture should be thick and creamy, rather like mayonnaise. Pesto is best served freshly made with cooked wholemeal pasta. These days, it is possible to buy fresh pasta, rather than dried, from many supermarkets and specialist delicatessens and this gives a more authentic dish.

Traditionally a pestle and mortar is used to mix this fragrant sauce, but a liquidiser can also be used. Fresh basil is an essential ingredient as is fresh Parmesan cheese.

Pesto

Per portion:

Calories 210

Fat 23g

Fibre 0g

Greek salad; Pesto with wholemeal fresh pasta; Green salad (above)

GREEK SALAD

SERVES 4

450g/1 lb ripe tomatoes, sliced
1 small onion, sliced into rings
½ cucumber, sliced
225g/8oz feta cheese, diced
100g/4oz black olives, stoned
1 teaspoon chopped fresh basil
3 tablespoons olive oil
1 teaspoon lemon juice

Preparation time **15 minutes**

1 Place the tomato, onion and cucumber in a bowl.
2 Arrange the cheese and olives on top of the salad.
3 Shake the basil, olive oil and lemon juice together and pour over the salad. Serve at once.

Feta cheese adds the distinctive flavour to this bright and colourful summer salad.

GREEN SALAD

SERVES 4

1 large Cos or Webb's Wonder lettuce
or 2 small round lettuces
2 bunches of watercress
box of mustard and cress or alfalfa
sprouts, or 100g/4oz mung
beansprouts
½ cucumber, sliced
1 green pepper, deseeded and sliced
4 spring onions, chopped
1 tablespoon white wine vinegar or
cider vinegar
3 tablespoons olive or sunflower oil
pinch of mustard powder
freshly ground black pepper
1 tablespoon chopped chives or parsley

Preparation time **20 minutes**

1 Wash the lettuce well, removing any coarse or yellowing leaves. Cut the leaves into smaller pieces if using Cos or Webb's Wonder. Place in a salad bowl.
2 Trim any yellowing leaves from the watercress. Add to the bowl. Trim the roots from the mustard and cress, if using. Add to the bowl, or add the beansprouts.
3 Add the cucumber, pepper and spring onions.
4 In a screw-topped jar, shake together the vinegar, oil, mustard, pepper and chives or parsley. Pour over the salad and toss together thoroughly. Serve at once as the leaves soon go soggy in the dressing.

There is nothing more attractive than a fresh, crispy green salad served on a warm summer's day. Take the trouble to add more interesting 'greenery' for a more exciting taste. Don't forget watercress either as it is an excellent source of iron and B vitamins.

Green salad

Per portion:

Calories 120

Fat 11g

Fibre 2g

Greek salad

Per portion:

Calories 260

Fat 18g

Fibre 3g

Paella

Per portion:
Calories 340
Fat 8g
Fibre 7g

Freezing and Microwave note
Paella can be frozen either in a rigid, airtight container or in a polythene bag, sealed. Defrost in the microwave for 20 minutes, then turn up to full power and reheat for 8 minutes.

PAELLA

SERVES 4

*225g/8oz French beans
2 tablespoons olive oil
175g/6oz onion, chopped
2 cloves garlic, crushed
225g/8oz tomatoes, peeled and chopped
generous pinch of turmeric or saffron
225g/8oz mushrooms, sliced
275g/10oz long-grain brown rice
600ml/1 pint vegetable stock plus
150ml/¼ pint dry cider (or use all vegetable stock)
freshly ground black pepper*

Preparation time **10 minutes**
Cooking time **35 minutes**

1 Trim the beans and cut into 1-cm/½-in lengths.
2 Place the oil in a paella pan or large frying pan with a lid or in a large heavy-based saucepan. Stir in the onions, garlic and tomatoes, and cook gently for 5 minutes, covered.
3 Add the turmeric and mushrooms, stirring in thoroughly. Cook for 1 minute. Add the rice and stir in well and cook for a further minute, before adding the stock, cider, if using, and beans. Bring to the boil, cover and reduce the heat. Let the mixture simmer for 25 minutes without disturbing. Test the rice to see if it is cooked. If the rice is ready and some liquid remains, then turn up the heat and cook to evaporate; if the rice is not cooked, cover again and let it cook gently until the grains are quite tender. Season to taste with black pepper and serve at once.

Paella is usually associated with shellfish and chicken, but traditional farmhouse-style paella is served without fish or poultry in a similar fashion to this recipe.

KEBABS

SERVES 4

*225g/8oz aubergine
sea salt
225g/8oz courgettes
1 red pepper, deseeded
1 green pepper, deseeded
2 small onions
8 button mushrooms
juice of ½ lemon
3 tablespoons olive oil
freshly ground black pepper
½ teaspoon dried or 1 teaspoon chopped fresh marjoram (optional)
1 clove garlic, crushed (optional)*

Paella; Kebabs

*Preparation time **45 minutes***
*Cooking time **20 minutes***

1 Slice the aubergine into 1-cm/½-in rings and sprinkle with salt. Leave for 30 minutes to draw out the bitterness. Pat dry and cut into cubes.

3 Cut the courgettes and peppers into 1-cm/½-in slices. Quarter the onions. Wipe the mushrooms.

3 Thread the prepared vegetables on to four long or eight short skewers.

4 Mix together the lemon juice, olive oil, pepper, marjoram and garlic, if using. Baste the kebabs with this mixture just before cooking on a barbecue or under a hot grill, and baste at frequent intervals during cooking too. Allow 10–20 minutes to cook, turning the skewers to ensure even cooking.

The flavour is best if the kebabs are cooked over a barbecue, but the recipe still works well when cooked under a hot grill.

Kebabs

Per portion:
Calories 140
Fat 11g
Fibre 3g

FRESH FRUIT SALAD

SERVES 4

$\frac{1}{2}$ honeydew melon · 2 oranges
100g/4oz white grapes
100g/4oz black grapes
2 peaches or nectarines
1 tablespoon Cointreau (optional)
3 tablespoons apple or orange juice
2 red-skinned dessert apples
juice of $\frac{1}{2}$ lemon · 1 banana
1 kiwi fruit (optional)

Preparation time **25 minutes, plus 3 hours to chill (optional)**

Fresh fruit salad

Per portion:	
Calories 160	
Fat 0g	
Fibre 6g	

1 Cut the flesh of the melon away from the skin and remove the seeds. Dice and place in a large glass bowl, with any juice.
2 Peel the orange and remove any pith. Cut into segments and cut each segment in four. Add to the bowl, with any juice.
3 Halve the grapes and remove the pips. Add the grapes to the bowl. Cut the peaches or nectarines in half, remove the stones and chop the flesh. Add to the bowl with the Cointreau, if using, and apple or orange juice. Mix thoroughly, cover and chill if liked, for up to 3 hours. Alternatively proceed at once and omit the chilling stage.
4 Cut the apples into quarters, remove the core and either slice finely or dice the flesh. Toss in the lemon juice. Peel the banana and slice thinly. Add to the apples and then to the bowl. Finally, peel the kiwi fruit, if using, slice thinly, halve slices and arrange on top of the fruit salad.

Variations

The most versatile of all desserts, fresh fruit salad can be varied according to the fruit available. It can be an inexpensive dish using cheap produce which is in season, like apples, oranges, peaches, pears, nectarines, melon, with perhaps a few strawberries or raspberries added for extra colour. Fresh fruit salad can also be served with the addition of one or more of the exotic fruits now readily available in this country: papaya (or pawpaw), mango, guava, kiwi fruit, kumquats or chunks of fresh pineapple.

Fruit salads based on a colour theme

Fresh fruit salad

add an unusual touch. A red salad can include strawberries, raspberries, cherries and perhaps some black grapes; or a dramatic orange salad can contain oranges, peaches, nectarines, mango, papaya, a red-skinned dessert apple and some delicately coloured Galia melon. A pale and interesting fruit salad can consist of kiwi fruit, white grapes, pears, green-skinned dessert apples, banana and honeydew melon.

Many recipes for fruit salads are based on a sugar syrup but fresh fruit is really sweet enough as it is and needs no extra sugar. Usually some extra fluid needs to be added to keep the fruits from drying out. This can be made up with any juice remaining after the fruit has been prepared plus some fresh orange, lemon or apple juice. A dash of Cointreau or a sweet white dessert wine adds extra flavour, and the fruit salad is best left to macerate for an hour or more (do not add fruits like apple and banana until the last minute as they will discolour).

As well as providing a crisp, colourful and refreshing finish to a meal, fresh fruit salad is very good nutritionally. It contains lots of vitamin C, fibre, other vital vitamins and minerals, hardly any fat and only the naturally occurring sugars. Serve it on its own or with some natural yogurt. Avoid adding extra fat in the form of cream.

Strawberry choux puffs

STRAWBERRY CHOUX PUFFS

SERVES 4

150 ml/¼ pint water
50 g/2 oz soft vegetable margarine
65 g/2½ oz 85% plain wheatmeal flour, sifted
2 free-range eggs
225 g/8 oz strawberries or raspberries
350 ml/12 fl oz strained, Greek-style yogurt

Preparation time **25 minutes**
Cooking time **25 minutes**
Oven temperature **220 C, 425 F, gas 7**
190 C, 375 F, gas 5

1 Place the water and margarine in a large saucepan and heat gently. When the margarine has melted turn up the heat and let the mixture come to the boil. Quickly add the flour, beat in and remove from heat. Continue to beat until the mixture is smooth and glossy and leaves the sides of the pan without sticking.
2 Cool slightly. Beat in one egg thoroughly and when it has been totally mixed in, add the second and beat thoroughly.
3 Place heaped teaspoonsful of the mixture on to two lightly oiled baking trays and bake for 15 minutes. Then reduce the oven temperature and cook for a further 10 minutes or until the pastry is completely cooked. Test by pressing the sides of the puffs; if they give, they need a little longer. When quite firm to the touch, remove from the oven and slit the side of each puff to let the steam escape; return to the oven to finally dry out for a further 5 minutes. Place on wire racks and leave to cool completely.
4 Hull the fruit and chop roughly, reserving a few whole strawberries or raspberries for decoration. Mix with the yogurt and use this mixture to fill the puffs. Pile up on a plate, decorating with the reserved fruit, halved if using strawberries.

A delicious version of that favourite dessert, profiteroles; calorie-rich chocolate sauce is replaced with fresh strawberries or raspberries. Greek yogurt is used in place of the cream.

Variations
This basic recipe for choux puffs can be varied by adding different fillings, either savoury or sweet. Although strawberries or raspberries give the prettiest effect for dessert, the sweet filling could be varied by adding different fruits to the yogurt.

Savoury choux puffs: *the choux puffs can be transformed into a savoury dish, ideal for a starter or buffet. Mix a crushed clove of garlic with 2 finely chopped spring onions and a finely diced 5-cm/2-in piece of cucumber to the yogurt and use as a filling.*
Garnish the puffs with cucumber slices and a sprinkling of chives. If using choux pastry for a savoury dish add a dash of mustard powder or cayenne pepper to the flour. For a richer pastry, stir in 25–50 g/1–2 oz finely grated Cheddar cheese to the mixture after the eggs.

Banana and kiwi fruit puffs: *mix mashed banana with the yogurt and decorate the puffs with sliced kiwi fruit.*

Pineapple puffs: *add chopped fresh pineapple to the yogurt and decorate with slices or chunks of fresh pineapple.*

Cherry puffs: *use stoned cherries instead of the strawberries or raspberries. Decorate with cherries on stalks.*

Apricot puffs: *peel and stone fresh apricots, then roughly chop them to use instead of the strawberries or raspberries.*

Peach and raspberry puffs: *peel, stone and chop fresh peaches, then use with half raspberries for the filling.*

Summer fruit puffs: *use a mixture of strawberries, raspberries and cherries in the filling.*

Strawberry choux puffs

Per portion:

Calories 260

Fat 14g

Fibre 2g

Freezing note
Choux pastry can be frozen successfully. Leave the puffs to cool before placing in a strong polythene bag, securing tightly and freezing. Defrost at room temperature.

HERB AND ONION TWISTS

MAKES 8

*350 g/12 oz plain wholemeal flour
1 teaspoon sea salt
15 g/½ oz fresh yeast
1 (25-mg) vitamin C tablet
2 tablespoons olive oil
200 ml/7 fl oz tepid water
100 g/4 oz onion, finely chopped or
grated
½ teaspoon chopped fresh or dried
rosemary
¼ teaspoon chopped fresh or dried
thyme
freshly ground black pepper
1 free-range egg, beaten, to glaze
poppy seeds to garnish*

*Preparation time **1 hour**
Cooking time **10–12 minutes**
Oven temperature **230 C, 450 F, gas 8***

1 Place the flour and salt in a large mixing bowl. Crumble the yeast into a jug and add the crushed vitamin C tablet, 1 tablespoon of the oil and the water. Stir well until the yeast has dissolved, then pour on to the flour.
2 Mix, using your hands to draw the dough together. Turn the dough out on to a lightly floured surface and knead for 6–8 minutes or until smooth. Cover and leave to rest for 10 minutes.
3 Heat the oven to 230C, 450F, gas 8. Lightly cook the onion and herbs in the remaining oil for 5 minutes, then remove from the heat.
4 Pull out the dough into an oblong and knead the onion mixture into it, adding a little extra flour to keep the dough smooth. Divide into eight equal portions and roll each piece into a long thin strip. Twist the strips into spirals. Place well apart on a lightly greased baking tray and cover. Put in a warm place to prove until doubled in size and springy to the touch.
5 Glaze with beaten egg, sprinkle with poppy seeds and bake at the top of the oven for 10–12 minutes, until golden brown. Cool on a wire rack or serve freshly baked.

Herb and onion twists

Per twist:

Calories 190

Fat 5g

Fibre 4g

PEANUT BUTTER PLAIT

MAKES 12 SLICES

450 g/1 lb plain wholemeal flour
1 teaspoon sea salt
15 g/½ oz soft vegetable margarine
25 g/1 oz fresh yeast
1 (25-mg) vitamin C tablet
150 ml/¼ pint skimmed milk
150 ml/¼ pint water
1 teaspoon honey
3 tablespoons peanut butter
1 free-range egg, beaten, to glaze
1 tablespoon chopped peanuts to garnish

*Preparation time **55–60 minutes***
*Cooking time **25–30 minutes***
*Oven temperature **230 C, 450 F, gas 8***

1 Place the flour and salt in a large mixing bowl and rub in the margarine.
2 Crumble the yeast into a jug. Crush the vitamin C tablet and add it to the yeast. Heat the milk and water in a saucepan until just warm, then pour on to the yeast and stir in the honey.
3 When the yeast has dissolved stir in the peanut butter and continue stirring until smooth. Pour on to the flour mixture and use your hands to mix into a dough. Turn the dough out on to a lightly floured surface and knead for 6–8 minutes until smooth. Cover and leave to rest for 10 minutes.
4 Have ready a lightly oiled baking tray and heat the oven to 230 C, 450 F, gas 8. Knead the dough lightly then divide into three equal pieces. Roll each piece out to a strip about 38 cm/15 in long. Join the three strips at one end and plait them loosely together.
5 Place the plait on the baking tray and cover. Leave to rise in a warm place for 30 minutes or until doubled in size.
6 Glaze the plait with beaten egg and sprinkle with the chopped peanuts. Bake in the centre of the oven for 25–30 minutes or until browned. When cooked, the loaf should sound hollow when tapped underneath. Transfer to a wire rack and leave to cool.

Peanut butter plait	
Per slice:	
Calories 170	
Fat 5g	
Fibre 4g	

Herb and onion twists;
Peanut butter plait

AUTUMN

SEPTEMBER · OCTOBER · NOVEMBER

Autumn is a season of contrast in fresh foods: September sees plums, damsons, blackberries and greengages at their best with the new season's apples and pears arriving in quick succession as the month progresses. By the end of November, however, it is the imported satsumas, clementines and oranges which are best value. Summer's courgettes, marrows and corn-on-the-cob are plentiful in early autumn, but by the end of the season the first of winter's root crops – swedes, carrots, turnips and parsnips – are best value and in plentiful supply. Cabbages and cauliflower are also good value now and Brussels sprouts also come into season at this time.

AUTUMN MENUS

1

Waldorf salad with hot wholemeal bread

Swede and leek roulade with roast potatoes and carrots

Fresh fruit

2

Pears with soft cheese and almonds

Cannellini goulash with long-grain brown rice and broccoli

Baked apples with yogurt

3

Rosy beet soup

Hazelnut-stuffed marrow

Fresh fruit

PUMPKIN SOUP

SERVES 4

450 g/1 lb pumpkin
1 tablespoon sunflower oil
100 g/4 oz onion, chopped
½ teaspoon ground cumin
pinch of cayenne
450 ml/¾ pint vegetable stock
1 bay leaf
freshly ground black pepper

Preparation time **10 minutes**
Cooking time **35 minutes**

1 Cut the flesh of the pumpkin away from the skin, discard the seeds and chop the flesh roughly.

2 Place the oil in a large saucepan and add the onion. Cook gently for 2 minutes. Stir in the spices and chopped pumpkin and cook for a further 2 minutes.

3 Add the stock and bay leaf. Bring to the boil, cover and simmer for 25 minutes.

4 Discard the bay leaf. Blend in a liquidiser to a smooth purée. Reheat, seasoning with black pepper to taste. Serve with croûtons if you wish.

Low in calories, pumpkin makes a good base for a light golden coloured soup.

Microwave note

Place the oil and onion in a large bowl and cook on maximum power for 2 minutes. Stir in the spices and pumpkin and cook for 2 minutes. Add the stock and cook for 10 minutes. Proceed as recipe.

Pumpkin soup

Pumpkin soup

Per portion:

Calories **60**

Fat **4g**

Fibre **2g**

Rosy beet soup

Per portion:

Calories 100

Fat 4g

Fibre 4g

Rosy beet soup

ROSY BEET SOUP

SERVES 4

1 tablespoon sunflower oil
100 g/4 oz onion, chopped
100 g/4 oz potato, diced
1 celery stick, chopped
350 g/12 oz whole uncooked beetroot,
peeled and diced
225 g/8 oz tomatoes, peeled and
chopped, or 1 (225-g/8-oz) can
tomatoes
900 ml/1½ pints vegetable stock
2 tablespoons cider vinegar
2 bay leaves
freshly ground black pepper
4 tablespoons natural yogurt

Preparation time **15 minutes**
Cooking time **1 hour 25 minutes**

1 Heat the oil in a large saucepan and add the onion, potato and celery. Cook gently for 2 minutes. Add the beetroot and cook for a further 3 minutes.

2 Stir in the tomatoes, stock, cider vinegar and bay leaves and bring to the boil. Reduce the heat and simmer for 1¼ hours or until the beetroot is quite soft.

3 Discard the bay leaves. Blend the soup in a liquidiser to a smooth purée. Reheat gently, seasoning with black pepper to taste. Garnish each serving with a swirl of yogurt.

Beetroot is a good source of B vitamins, many minerals and fibre and deserves to be made more of in the diet. This soup is ideal for chilly autumn days. It is important to add the vinegar; without the acid the beetroot will cook to a strange brown colour.

Freezing and Microwave note
Freeze in a firm container after blending in a liquidiser. Defrost at room temperature or in the microwave on defrost setting for 15 minutes. Reheat on full power for 8 minutes or until hot. Season and garnish as recipe.

Apple and Stilton popovers

Per portion:

Calories	430
Fat	28g
Fibre	6g

APPLE AND STILTON POPOVERS

SERVES 4

Pastry
175 g/6 oz plain wholemeal flour
75 g/3 oz soft vegetable margarine
cold water to mix
Filling
50 g/2 oz onion, grated
225 g/8 oz cooking apple, peeled, cored and grated
75 g/3 oz Stilton cheese, grated
Glaze
1 free-range egg, beaten
1 tablespoon sesame seeds

Preparation time **30 minutes, plus 15 minutes to chill**
Cooking time **20 minutes**
Oven temperature **200 C, 400 F, gas 6**

1 Sift the flour into a mixing bowl and add the bran from the sieve. Rub in the margarine until the mixture resembles fine breadcrumbs. Place the bowl in the refrigerator to rest for 15 minutes.
2 Mix together the onion, apple and Stilton.
3 Add just enough cold water to the flour and margarine mixture to mix to a soft dough. Divide into four. Roll out each quarter on a lightly floured surface and cut out a 13-cm/5-in circle. Dampen the edges with a pastry brush and divide the filling between the four circles, placing on one half of the circle and folding the remaining half over. Seal the edges and flute with a knife. Make three slits to let the steam escape. Place on a baking tray, glaze with egg and scatter sesame seeds on top. Bake for 15–20 minutes.

Stilton is a cheese to be reserved for special occasions – not only is it quite expensive, but it is also one of the fattiest cheeses. However, with its rich flavour a little goes a long way as in this unusual first course. Serve with a salad garnish.

Apple and Stilton popovers; Pears with soft cheese and almonds

PEARS WITH SOFT CHEESE AND ALMONDS

SERVES 4

4 small or 2 large ripe Comice pears
100g/4oz low-fat soft cheese
25g/1oz ground almonds
shredded lettuce
50g/2oz flaked almonds

*Preparation time **15 minutes***
*Cooking time **30 minutes***

1 Wipe the pears and halve. Remove the cores.
2 Blend the soft cheese with the ground almonds and pile into the cavities of the pears. Arrange on a bed of shredded lettuce.
3 Toast the flaked almonds for 2–3 minutes under a hot grill and sprinkle on top of the pears. Serve at once, before the pears have a chance to brown.

Few people consider serving pears as a first course, but this recipe makes a really attractive starter. Choose home-grown, plump Comice pears for best results.

Pears with soft cheese and almonds

Per portion:

Calories 160

Fat 12g

Fibre 4g

SPICY LENTIL PÂTÉ

SERVES 4

*100 g/4 oz red lentils, soaked in
boiling water for 1 hour
250 ml/8 fl oz water
1 bay leaf
1 tablespoon sunflower oil
100 g/4 oz onion, finely chopped
½ teaspoon ground turmeric
½ teaspoon ground cumin
175 g/6 oz carrot, finely grated
freshly ground black pepper
1 tablespoon natural yogurt
fresh coriander leaves or parsley to
garnish*

Preparation time **10 minutes plus
1 hour soaking**
Cooking time **45 minutes**

I Drain the lentils and place in a pan with the water and bay leaf. Cover, bring to the boil then simmer for 35–40 minutes until soft. Remove from heat and discard the bay leaf. Mash to a purée.

2 Heat the oil in a saucepan and cook the onion over a low heat for 2 minutes, then add the spices and grated carrot and cook for a further 2 minutes.

3 Stir into the cooked lentils and season with black pepper. Allow to cool before stirring in the yogurt.

4 Divide between 4 ramekin dishes and garnish with coriander leaves or parsley. Serve with wholemeal toast.

Lentils are one of the few pulses to cook more quickly and successfully in the microwave and this tasty pâté can be cooked this way, if preferred.

Microwave note

To prepare the pâté in the microwave, place the lentils, water and bay leaf in an ovenproof casserole and cook on full power for 12 minutes until the lentils are quite soft. Remove the bay leaf, mash to a purée and then cook the onion in the oil on full power for 2 minutes; add the spices and carrot and cook for 2 minutes. Follow recipe as detailed.

Spicy lentil pâté	
Per portion:	
Calories 130	
Fat 4g	
Fibre 5g	

STUFFED TOMATOES

SERVES 4

4 large ripe tomatoes
175 g/6 oz low-fat soft cheese
2 celery sticks, finely sliced
50 g/2 oz walnuts, finely chopped
freshly ground black pepper
chopped parsley to garnish

---

*Preparation time **20 minutes plus 1 hour to chill***
*Cooking time (optional) **15 minutes***
*Oven temperature (optional) **200 C, 400 F, gas 6***

---

1 Cut the tops off the tomatoes and scoop out all the flesh. Discard the seeds and chop the remainder. Mix with the soft cheese, celery, walnuts and season with black pepper to taste.
2 Place the mixture back inside the tomato shells, replace the lids and garnish with the parsley. Chill for 1 hour and serve cold.
3 To serve hot, if liked, bake in the oven for 15 minutes.

Walnuts and celery make a tasty filling with plenty of crunch and the low-fat soft cheese helps to keep the calories low.

Stuffed tomatoes	
Per portion:	
Calories 100	
Fat 7g	
Fibre 2g	

Spicy lentil pâté; Stuffed tomatoes

LEEK GOUGÈRE

SERVES 4

Pastry
150 ml/¼ pint cold water
50 g/2 oz soft vegetable margarine
*65 g/2½ oz 85% plain wheatmeal flour,
sifted*
2 free-range eggs
50 g/2 oz Gruyère cheese, finely grated
pinch of mustard powder
Filling
575 g/1¼ lb leeks
20 g/¾ oz soft vegetable margarine
20 g/¾ oz 85% plain wheatmeal flour
250 ml/8 fl oz skimmed milk
freshly ground black pepper

*Preparation time **30 minutes***
*Cooking time **40 minutes***
*Oven temperature **220 C, 425 F, gas 7***
190 C, 375 F, gas 5

1 Lightly oil a gratin dish or similar shallow oval, ovenproof dish.
2 Place the water and margarine in a pan and heat until the margarine has melted. Turn up the heat to let the mixture boil, then quickly add the flour. Beat in well and remove from the heat. Continue beating until the mixture is smooth and glossy and leaves the sides of the pan.
3 Cool slightly. Add one egg and beat in thoroughly before adding the second. Beat well, add the Gruyère and mustard.
4 Pipe or spoon rosettes of the mixture around the edge of the dish. Bake for 20 minutes. Reduce the oven temperature and continue to cook for a further 10 minutes.
5 While the pastry is baking, prepare the filling. Trim away the roots and coarse leaves from the leeks. Cut into 1-cm/½-in slices and plunge into a small amount of boiling water. Cook for 6–8 minutes. Drain, reserving the cooking liquid.
6 Melt the margarine and stir in the flour. Cook for 1 minute. Gradually add the milk and enough of the cooking liquid from the leeks to make a fairly thick sauce. Add the leeks and season with pepper. Simmer until the pastry is ready, pour into the centre of the dish and serve.

Adding cheese to choux pastry makes a tasty base for a creamy sauce.

CAULIFLOWER AND PASTA SUPREME

SERVES 4

100 g/4 oz wholemeal pasta shapes
2 leeks · 1 large cauliflower
25 g/1 oz soft vegetable margarine
100 g/4 oz button mushrooms
25 g/1 oz 85% plain wheatmeal flour
300 ml/½ pint skimmed milk
100 g/4 oz Cheddar cheese, grated
freshly ground black pepper
2 tablespoons sesame seeds

*Preparation time **25 minutes***
*Cooking time **35 minutes***

1 Cook the pasta in boiling water for 10–12 minutes until just tender. Drain.
2 Trim the leeks and cut into 1-cm/½-in slices. Cut the cauliflower into florets and place both in a small amount of boiling water in a large pan. Cook for about 8 minutes. Drain, reserving the cooking water. Transfer the vegetables to a flameproof casserole and keep warm.
3 Melt the margarine in a pan, add the mushrooms and cook for 2–3 minutes, then stir in the flour. Stirring constantly, add the milk and enough of the cooking water from the vegetables to make a smooth sauce. Add two-thirds of the cheese and simmer. Season with pepper. Stir in the pasta and heat through.
4 Light the grill and pour the sauce over the vegetables. Top with the remaining Cheddar and the sesame seeds and grill until a bubbling golden brown.

Wholemeal pasta and extra vegetables add protein to the good old favourite, cauliflower cheese, and turn this into a perfectly balanced complete meal.

Leek gougère

Per portion:

Calories 360

Fat 21g

Fibre 6g

Cauliflower & pasta supreme

Per portion:

Calories 330

Fat 12g

Fibre 10g

Freezing note
Choux pastry freezes well but gougère itself is not an ideal dish for freezing. One alternative, using the same ingredients, would be to make individual choux puffs. Wrap the completely cooled choux puffs in polythene bags and freeze until required. They are best defrosted at room temperature, filled and then reheated in the oven for 10 minutes.

Microwave note

At stage 3, melt the margarine in a large casserole dish on full power for 30 seconds. Stir in the flour and cook for 30 seconds. Add the milk and heat for 2 minutes. Gradually add the stock and beat well. Add the mushrooms and cheese and cook for 2 minutes. Add the pasta and heat through for 1 minute. Proceed as recipe.

Leek gougère; Cauliflower and pasta supreme

Leek and bean crumble

Per portion:	
Calories 480	
Fat 30g	
Fibre 13g	

Microwave note

The filling can easily be prepared in the microwave. Place the trimmed and sliced leeks with the chopped celery and margarine in a covered dish and cook on full power for 5 minutes. Add the mushrooms and cook for 2 minutes. Stir in the flour and cook for 1 minute. Now heat the milk, water and stock for 3 minutes and gradually stir into the leek mixture. Season with black pepper and then cook on full power for 4 minutes. Stir in the butter beans and heat through for 1 minute. Proceed as above. The crumble can also be reheated in the microwave on full power for 4 minutes.

LEEK AND BEAN CRUMBLE

SERVES 4

Crumble
65 g/2½ oz soft vegetable margarine
115 g/4½ oz plain wholemeal flour
50 g/2 oz walnuts, finely chopped or ground

Filling
450 g/1 lb leeks, trimmed and finely sliced
40 g/1½ oz soft vegetable margarine
1 celery stick, finely sliced
75 g/3 oz button mushrooms, sliced
20 g/¾ oz wheatmeal flour
300 ml/½ pint skimmed milk
3 tablespoons hot water mixed with ¼ teaspoon Vecon stock concentrate
freshly ground black pepper
75 g/3 oz dried butter beans, cooked or 1 small can of butter beans, drained

Preparation time **15 minutes**
Cooking time **30 minutes**
Oven temperature **190 C, 375 F, gas 5**

1 To make the crumble. Rub the margarine into the flour until the mixture resembles fine breadcrumbs. Stir in the chopped or ground walnuts. Set aside.
2 Place the leeks in a pan with one inch of boiling water in the base and cook for 5–8 minutes until just tender. Drain.
3 Melt the margarine in another saucepan and cook the celery gently for 2 minutes. Stir in the sliced mushrooms and cook for a further 2 minutes.
4 Add the flour and mix to a smooth paste. Gradually add the milk and Vecon stock and bring to the boil. Lower heat to simmer and stir in the leeks and butter beans, seasoning with black pepper to taste.
5 Pour the sauce into the base of an ovenproof dish or four small ramekins and top with the crumble mixture. Bake for 12 minutes and serve at once.

The beans and crumble provide a good source of protein in this flavoursome dish. For a change you may like to try adding a can of chick peas.

VEGETABLE OMELETTE SPECIALS

MAKES 4

2 tablespoons sunflower oil
100 g/4 oz onion, finely chopped
175 g/6 oz button mushrooms, finely chopped
½ green pepper, finely chopped or 4 tablespoons sweetcorn kernels (optional)
8 free-range eggs
8 tablespoons cold water
¼ teaspoon fresh or ½ teaspoon dried thyme
freshly ground black pepper
100 g/4 oz Cheddar or Double Gloucester cheese, finely grated

*Preparation time **10 minutes***
*Cooking time **5 minutes plus 5 minutes each***

1 Heat the oil in an omelette pan and cook the onion for 2 minutes, over a low heat without browning. Stir in the mushrooms and continue to cook until the juices run.

2 Stir in the chopped pepper or sweetcorn, if using, and cook 1 minute more. Remove from heat and place mixture in a bowl. Preheat the grill.

3 Make each omelette, fresh, in turn. Take two eggs and beat lightly with 2 tablespoons cold water and a pinch of thyme. Season with black pepper to taste.

4 Take one quarter of the mushroom mixture and place in the base of the omelette pan. Heat through. Pour in the beaten egg and tip the pan so that the base is covered evenly. As the mixture starts to set, gently lift a little away from the edges all round and tip more mixture in. Repeat until the mixture is set.

5 Cook for 1 minute, then sprinkle one quarter of the cheese on top and place under the heated grill. Cook until the cheese has melted and the omelette has risen slightly. Slide at once onto a warmed plate and serve immediately. Repeat with the other 3 omelettes.

Eggs have acquired rather an unhealthy reputation lately because of their high cholesterol content, but if eaten in moderation (up to 4 a week) they can play an important part in a healthy vegetarian diet, as they are an excellent source of protein, vital vitamins and minerals, especially B vitamins and iron. Omelettes made with the tasty addition of lightly cooked vegetables are a fast and easy supper dish. Just serve with wholemeal bread.

Omelettes

Per omelette:

Calories 360

Fat 28g

Fibre 1g

Omelette; Leek and butter bean crumble

SWEDE AND LEEK ROULADE

SERVES 4

225 g/8 oz swede, peeled and diced
2 tablespoons skimmed milk
freshly ground black pepper
3 large free-range eggs
Filling
225 g/8 oz leeks
25 g/1 oz unsalted butter or soft
vegetable margarine
25 g/1 oz plain wholemeal flour
200 ml/7 fl oz skimmed milk
freshly ground black pepper
curly endive to garnish
(optional)

Preparation time **25 minutes**
Cooking time **1 hour 10 minutes**
Oven temperature **200 C, 400 F, gas 6**

1 Line and grease a 23 × 33-cm/9 × 13-in Swiss roll tin.
2 Place the swede in a pan of cold water and bring to the boil, reduce the heat and simmer for 30–35 minutes or until really soft. Drain and mash with the milk and pepper to taste.

3 Prepare the filling. Trim the leeks and slice finely. Melt the butter or margarine over a low heat and add the leeks. Cover and cook gently for 10 minutes until the leeks are just soft.
4 Stir in the flour thoroughly and gradually add the milk, stirring well to form a smooth sauce. Season and set aside.
5 Separate the eggs. Beat the egg yolks into the mashed swede. Whisk the egg whites until they form stiff peaks and gently fold into the swede mixture with a metal spoon. Pour into the prepared tin and smooth the top. Bake for 15–20 minutes until just firm to the touch.
6 While the roulade is in the oven, reheat the leek sauce. Place a sheet of greaseproof paper on the worktop and as soon as the roulade is ready, invert on top of the paper and lift tin. Carefully peel off the paper – if it sticks place a damp cloth on top of the paper for a few seconds before trying again. Spread the leek sauce on top and quickly roll up like a Swiss roll, using the greaseproof paper as a guide. Slice and serve at once, garnished with curly endive, if preferred.

An attractive and light dish which transforms swede into something special.

Microwave note
The leek filling can be prepared in the microwave. Place the butter or margarine in a casserole dish with the sliced leeks and cook on full power for 5 minutes. Heat the milk on full power for 2 minutes. Stir the flour into the leeks and gradually add the milk. Season and heat in the microwave on full power for a further 3 minutes.

Swede and leek roulade

Swede and leek roulade

Per portion:	
Calories 180	
Fat 10g	
Fibre 4g	

Microwave note
The marrow can be cooked partially on full power. Arrange in a shallow dish and add 2 tablespoons cold water. Cover and cook on full power for 3 minutes. Proceed as recipe.

Hazelnut-stuffed courgettes

HAZELNUT-STUFFED MARROW

SERVES 4

1 medium marrow, or 675 g / 1½ lb courgettes
100 g / 4 oz wholemeal breadcrumbs
50 g / 2 oz hazelnuts, ground
50 g / 2 oz walnuts, ground
50 g / 2 oz onion, chopped
1 tablespoon oil
100 g / 4 oz button mushrooms, chopped
½ teaspoon chopped fresh sage
1 tablespoon chopped parsley
1 tablespoon tomato purée
1 free-range egg
freshly ground black pepper
50 g / 2 oz farmhouse Cheddar cheese, finely grated
2 teaspoons sesame seeds

Preparation time **25 minutes**
Cooking time **35 minutes**
Oven temperature **200 C, 400 F, gas 6**

1 Cut the marrow into four 2.5-cm / 1-in slices, or trim and halve the courgettes. Scoop out the seeds and plunge the rings or courgette halves into a pan of boiling water. Cook for 2 minutes; alternatively, steam for 5 minutes. Drain and set aside while preparing the filling.
2 Place the breadcrumbs, hazelnuts and walnuts in a mixing bowl. Cook the onion in the oil for 2 minutes without browning. Add the mushrooms to the pan. Heat through, then add to the mixing bowl.
3 Place the sage and parsley in the bowl and beat in the tomato purée and egg. Season with pepper.
4 Place the marrow rings or courgette halves in an ovenproof dish. Arrange the stuffing in the centre of each ring or half, pressing down firmly. Scatter the grated cheese and sesame seeds on top. Place 2 tablespoons cold water in the dish, cover with foil and bake for 30 minutes. Remove foil and bake uncovered for the final 5 minutes to brown. Serve at once.

Marrow is remarkably low in calories but tends to have rather a bland taste. This makes it the perfect vehicle for stuffing – as in these tasty and nutritious marrow rings. The alternative of courgettes, shown in our picture, is equally good.

Hazelnut-stuffed marrow

Per portion:
Calories 340
Fat 22g
Fibre 9g

LAYERED NUT TERRINE

SERVES 4

*100 g/4 oz carrots, scrubbed and cut
into 2.5-cm/1-in matchsticks
100 g/4 oz courgettes, cut into 2.5-cm/
1-in matchsticks
150 g/5 oz wholemeal breadcrumbs
175 g/6 oz ground hazelnuts
100 g/4 oz onion, finely chopped
100 g/4 oz button mushrooms, finely
chopped
1 celery stick, finely chopped
2 tablespoons finely chopped parsley
$\frac{1}{2}$ teaspoon finely chopped fresh thyme
3 free-range eggs, separated
$\frac{1}{4}$ teaspoon yeast extract
4 tablespoons boiling water
freshly ground black pepper*

Preparation time **25 minutes**
Cooking time **1 hour**
Oven temperature **200 C, 400 F, gas 6**

1 Blanch the carrots in boiling water for 5 minutes. Add the courgettes and blanch for 1 minute. Drain and set aside.
2 Line a 1-kg/2-lb loaf tin with grease-proof paper. Place the breadcrumbs and ground hazelnuts in a large mixing bowl and add the onion, mushrooms, celery, parsley and thyme. Add the egg yolks to the mixing bowl.
3 Dissolve the yeast extract in the boiling water and add to the bowl. Mix in thoroughly, seasoning with black pepper.
4 Stiffly whisk the egg whites and gently fold into the nut mixture.
5 Place one-third of the mixture in the base of the prepared loaf tin and arrange the carrot sticks on top in three neat lines. Cover with another third of the nut mixture, spreading evenly, and add the courgettes in neat lines. Cover with another third of the nut mixture, smoothing the top.
6 Bake in the centre of the oven for about 50 minutes. Carefully turn the terrine out of the tin, cut into eight slices. Serve hot.

This crunchy nut terrine can be served

Layered nut terrine

Per portion:

Calories 330

Fat 21g

Fibre 7g

Microwave note
The stuffed cabbage leaves can also be baked in the microwave on full power for 8 minutes. Do not use foil to cover.

with roast potatoes, parsnips and a green vegetable. Make a vegetarian gravy with vegetable stock, a little cornflour and season well, then serve separately.

STUFFED CABBAGE LEAVES

SERVES 4

*1 medium aubergine
sea salt
1 tablespoon sunflower oil
100 g/4 oz onion, finely chopped
1 clove garlic, crushed
150 g/5 oz long-grain brown rice
150 ml/$\frac{1}{4}$ pint dry white wine
150 ml/$\frac{1}{4}$ pint vegetable stock
3 tomatoes, peeled and chopped
75 g/3 oz mushrooms, sliced
2 tablespoons chopped parsley
$\frac{1}{2}$ teaspoon fresh basil or marjoram
freshly ground black pepper
few extra tablespoons vegetable stock
1 large Savoy or other green cabbage*

*Preparation time **20 minutes plus 30
minutes to stand***
*Cooking time **1 hour***
*Oven temperature **190 C, 375 F, gas 5***

1 Dice the aubergine and sprinkle with
sea salt. Leave to stand for 30 minutes to
draw out the bitter juices. Pat dry.
2 Heat the oil in a saucepan and cook
the onion and garlic gently for 2 minutes
over a low heat. Stir in the rice and cook
for 1 minute until the grains turn transparent.
3 Stir in the wine, stock, tomatoes,
mushrooms and aubergine. Bring to the
boil, cover, reduce heat and simmer for
25–30 minutes until the rice is tender
and the liquid is absorbed.
4 Add the parsley and basil and season
with black pepper to taste.
5 Discarding any yellowing or coarse
outer leaves, remove 12 good-sized
leaves from the cabbage and plunge into
a pan of boiling water and blanch for 2
minutes. This helps to soften the leaves,
making them easier to roll up. Drain.

6 When filling is cooked, divide between the leaves and carefully roll up.
Place in a shallow ovenproof dish and
spoon some vegetable stock in the base,
using just enough to cover the base of
the dish and prevent the leaves from
sticking. Cover with foil and bake for 20
minutes in the centre of the oven. Serve
with baked potatoes.

*Aubergines are often good value in the
autumn and they are used in this recipe
to make a tasty stuffing for cabbage
leaves. Traditionally vine leaves are
used, but cabbage leaves are cheaper
and more readily available.*

Stuffed cabbage leaves

Per portion:
Calories 240
Fat 4g
Fibre 8g

Cannellini goulash

Per portion:

Calories 210

Fat 4g

Fibre 16g

Chick-peas with tomatoes

Per portion:

Calories 140

Fat 0g

Fibre 11g

CANNELLINI GOULASH

SERVES 4

*100 g/4 oz onion, chopped
1 celery stick, chopped
175 g/6 oz carrots, scrubbed and diced
100 g/4 oz potato, scrubbed and diced
1 tablespoon sunflower oil
175 g/6 oz cannellini beans, soaked overnight
1 (425-g/15-oz) can tomatoes
600 ml/1 pint vegetable stock
1 red pepper, deseeded and chopped
1 tablespoon paprika
2 bay leaves
freshly ground black pepper
2 tablespoons natural yogurt*

*Preparation time **10 minutes, plus overnight soaking**
Cooking time **1 hour 35 minutes**
Oven temperature **190 C, 375 F, gas 5***

1 Cook the onion, celery, carrot and potato gently in the oil for 2 minutes. Add the drained beans, tomatoes, stock, pepper, paprika and bay leaves. Bring to the boil, transfer to an ovenproof dish and bake for 1½ hours or until the beans are tender. Season to taste and stir in the yogurt.

Cannellini beans, or white kidney beans as they are sometimes called, make a lovely addition to this rich and nutritious vegetable goulash. Serve with wholemeal pasta for a perfectly balanced intake of protein.

CHICK-PEAS WITH TOMATOES

SERVES 4

*1 tablespoon olive oil
100 g/4 oz onion, chopped
2 cloves garlic, crushed
225 g/8 oz potatoes, scrubbed and diced
¼ teaspoon ground cumin
1 red pepper, deseeded and chopped
175 g/6 oz courgettes, sliced
1 (425-g/15-oz) can tomatoes, chopped
1 (425-g/15-oz) can chick-peas, drained
1 tablespoon tomato purée
¼ teaspoon yeast extract
2 tablespoons cold water
freshly ground black pepper
1 tablespoon chopped parsley*

*Preparation time **15 minutes**
Cooking time **30 minutes***

1 Heat the oil in a large saucepan and add the onion, garlic and potatoes and cook gently for 2 minutes. Stir in the cumin and cook for a further minute.
2 Stir in the pepper, courgettes, tomatoes, chick-peas, tomato purée, yeast extract and the cold water. Bring to the boil, cover and simmer for 20–25 minutes until the potatoes are tender.
3 Season to taste with black pepper and stir in the parsley.

Chick-peas, like all pulses, are a good source of protein and fibre. Using canned chick-peas saves time in making this quick supper dish. Serve with couscous or with brown rice or wholemeal pasta.

Note

If serving with couscous, allow 225 g/ 8 oz for four servings. Traditionally, couscous is cooked in a specially designed couscousier, being steamed gently in the vapours from the sauce as it cooks below. If you do not have a couscousier, an equally tasty way of cooking couscous is to 'roast' it in a heavy-based frying pan without any fat for 2 minutes, then gradually add hot vegetable stock a little at a time, stirring constantly so the grains swell and absorb the stock. Continue in this way until the couscous is soft. Serve at once with the chick-pea and tomato sauce.

Cannellini goulash;
Chick-peas with tomatoes

Spiced black-eye beans;
Chilli beans

SPICED BLACK-EYE BEANS

SERVES 4

225 g/8 oz black-eye beans, soaked overnight
2 onions, finely chopped
I green chilli, finely chopped
2.5-cm/1-in fresh ginger, grated
2 black cardamoms
6 black peppercorns
2.5-cm/1-in piece cinnamon stick
6 cloves
600 ml/1 pint water
I tablespoon vegetable oil
4 cloves garlic, finely chopped
½ teaspoon paprika
I teaspoon turmeric
½ teaspoon ground cumin
2 teaspoons ground coriander
I tablespoon finely chopped coriander leaves
I teaspoon garam masala
3 tablespoons lemon juice

Preparation time **10 minutes plus overnight soaking**
Cooking time **70 minutes**

I Place beans in a saucepan with one onion, and add the chilli, ginger, cardamoms, peppercorns, cinnamon and cloves. Pour in the water.
2 Bring to the boil and then reduce the heat, cover and simmer for 55 minutes until tender. Drain and keep the stock.
3 Heat the oil in a saucepan and cook the remaining onion and garlic for 2 minutes. Add the paprika, turmeric, cumin and ground coriander, mixing together well.
4 Add the drained beans and stir gently. Mix in the coriander leaves, garam masala and lemon juice and then add sufficient stock to make a sauce, simmer gently for about 3 minutes and then serve with a rice dish.

A nutritious dish with a high fibre content and a delicious spicy flvour.

CHILLI BEANS

SERVES 4

2 tablespoons sunflower oil
225 g/8 oz onion, finely chopped
225 g/8 oz carrots, diced
I clove garlic, crushed
I celery stick, finely chopped
3 green chillies, deseeded and chopped
I red pepper, deseeded and chopped
I green pepper, deseeded and chopped
900 g/2 lb tomatoes, peeled and chopped or 2 (425-g/15-oz) cans tomatoes
225 g/8 oz red kidney beans, soaked overnight
½ teaspoon ground cumin
pinch cayenne
I bay leaf

Preparation time **15 minutes plus overnight soaking**
Cooking time **2–2¼ hours**
Oven temperature **180 C, 350 F, gas 4 (optional)**

I Heat the oil in a large saucepan and add the onion, carrots, garlic, celery and chillies and cook gently for 3 minutes.
2 Stir in the chopped peppers and tomatoes, drained beans, cumin, cayenne and bay leaf. Stir together thoroughly and bring to the boil. Cover and boil for 10 minutes. Reduce heat and simmer for 1¾–2 hours until the beans are soft.
3 Serve the beans with boiled long-grain brown rice and a crisp side salad.
4 Alternatively, after the mixture has been boiled for 10 minutes, it could be transferred to an ovenproof dish and baked slowly for 1¾–2 hours; cook baked potatoes at the same time, and serve them with the chilli.

Spiced black-eye beans

Per portion:

Calories 200

Fat 5g

Fibre 15g

Microwave note
Chilli beans improve in flavour if they are kept overnight. The dish can be reheated for a few minutes on full power in the microwave. The dish also freezes well and it can be defrosted on a defrost setting in the microwave oven. Allow about 7–10 minutes. Break up the block of beans as it thaws, then heat on full power for a few minutes.

Chilli beans

Per portion:

Calories 280

Fat 8g

Fibre 20g

99

Brazil bake; Tortilla

Microwave note

Nut roasts such as this can be cooked in the microwave to save time but they lack the appetising colour of roasts cooked more slowly in the oven. The microwave is, however, invaluable in reheating slices of nut roast; allow 2 minutes on full power for each portion.

Brazil bake	
Per portion:	
Calories 380	
Fat 27g	
Fibre 8g	

BRAZIL BAKE

SERVES 6

225 g/8 oz Brazil nuts
225 g/8 oz wholemeal breadcrumbs
225 g/8 oz carrots, scrubbed and grated
175 g/6 oz onion, chopped
3 celery sticks, sliced
1 red pepper, deseeded and chopped
1 teaspoon dried or 2 teaspoons fresh marjoram
freshly ground black pepper
3 free-range eggs
3 tablespoons tomato purée

Preparation time **25 minutes**
Cooking time **45 minutes**
Oven temperature **190 C, 375 F, gas 5**

1 Line and lightly oil a 20-cm/8-in ring tin or a 450-g/1-lb loaf tin. If using the loaf tin, the above quantities should be halved.
2 Grind the nuts or chop very finely. Mix with the breadcrumbs.
3 Mix together the carrot, onion, celery and pepper.
4 Add the marjoram and season with pepper. Beat in the eggs and tomato purée, adding a little water to mix.
5 Pile into the prepared ring mould or loaf tin and smooth down the top. Bake for 45 minutes. Serve hot or cold. Chopped fresh vegetables make a crunchy addition.

The combination of nuts and grains (wholemeal breadcrumbs) makes a well balanced protein dish.

and leave to cool before dicing.

2 Place the oil in a 15-cm/6-in omelette pan and heat. Add the potatoes and cook for 3–4 minutes to heat through.

3 Beat the eggs together in a jug and pour into the pan. Stir around to help them set evenly, but stop stirring when they are firming up. Run a palette knife around the edges to neaten and continue cooking to set the eggs. Flip the tortilla over to finish cooking and invert on to a plate. Season with pepper and garnish with parsley.

This traditional Spanish dish can be served hot, or can be left to cool and served with a side salad. If liked, add two fresh, peeled and chopped tomatoes to the potatoes in the pan for a more colourful dish.

TORTILLA

S E R V E S 4

225 g/8 oz potatoes
1½ tablespoons olive oil
4 free-range eggs
freshly ground black pepper
1 tablespoon chopped parsley to garnish

Preparation time **30 minutes**
Cooking time **25 minutes**

1 Scrub the potatoes and cut into 5-cm/2-in pieces. Place in a pan of cold water and bring to the boil. Reduce heat and simmer for 15 minutes until tender. Drain

Tortilla	
Per portion:	
Calories	190
Fat	12g
Fibre	1g

PASTIES

MAKES 4

Pastry
100 g| 4 oz plain wholemeal flour
50 g| 2 oz vegetable margarine
40 g| 1½ oz Cheddar cheese, grated
cold water to mix

Filling
25 g| 1 oz onion, finely chopped
1 tablespoon chopped celery
1 tablespoon sweetcorn kernels
(optional)
50 g| 2 oz potato, diced
75 g| 3 oz carrot, diced
1 tablespoon cold water
pinch mixed herbs

Glaze
skimmed milk
1 tablespoon sesame seeds

Preparation time **30 minutes plus 10 minutes to chill**
Cooking time **25–30 minutes**
Oven temperature **200 C, 400 F, gas 6**
180 C, 350 F, gas 4

1 Sift the flour into a bowl and rub in the margarine until the mixture resembles fine breadcrumbs. Stir in the grated cheese and chill for 10 minutes. Add just enough cold water to mix to a dough and divide into four pieces.
2 Roll each piece of dough out to a thin circle about the size of a small saucer. Lightly brush the edges with water.
3 Mix together all the filling ingredients in a bowl and divide the mixture between the four pasties, arranging in a strip down the centre of each. Bring the pastry edges together to meet over the filling. Pinch together, seal the edges and transfer to a lightly greased baking tray.
4 Glaze with milk and sprinkle the sesame seeds on top. Bake for 10 minutes then lower the heat and bake for a further 15–20 minutes.
5 Cool on a wire rack. The pasties will store in the refrigerator for two days.

These pasties make an ideal packed lunch, as they supply protein plus fibre, vitamins and minerals.

Pasties

Per portion:

Calories **240**

Fat **14g**

Fibre **3g**

ROOT VEGETABLE PIE

SERVES 4

Pastry
75 g| 3 oz plain wholemeal flour
40 g| 1½ oz soft vegetable margarine
25 g| 1 oz rolled oats
cold water to mix

Filling
1 tablespoon oil
50 g| 2 oz onion, finely chopped
½ celery stick, finely chopped
100 g| 4 oz turnip, peeled and diced
100 g| 4 oz parsnip, peeled and diced
225 g| 8 oz swede, peeled and diced
300 ml| ½ pint vegetable stock
freshly ground black pepper
2 teaspoons cornflour or arrowroot
3 tablespoons water
skimmed milk to glaze

*Preparation time **25 minutes plus 15 minutes to chill***
*Cooking time **35 minutes***
*Oven temperature **200 C, 400 F, gas 6***

1 Place the flour in a mixing bowl and rub in the margarine until mixture resembles fine breadcrumbs. Stir in the oats. Chill for 10–15 minutes.

2 Meanwhile prepare the filling. Heat the oil in a saucepan and cook the onion and celery for 2 minutes. Stir in the remaining vegetables, add the stock, season with black pepper to taste, and bring to the boil. Cover, reduce the heat and simmer for 8 minutes.

3 Mix the arrowroot with the water and add to the pan to thicken. Take off heat and reserve.

4 Add just enough cold water to the pastry mixture to make a soft dough and roll out on a lightly floured surface to a shape large enough to cover a greased, 600 ml/1 pint pie dish.

5 Place the filling in the dish and top with pastry. Trim the edges and roll out any leftover pastry to make decorations for the top. Glaze with milk, cut two slits to let the steam out and bake for 20 minutes until golden brown. Serve at once with roast or baked potatoes and a green vegetable.

A tasty pie making good use of cheap root vegetables. The addition of rolled oats to the pastry gives an interesting nutty flavour to the pastry topping.

Root vegetable pie
Per portion:
Calories 250
Fat 15g
Fibre 6g

Pasty; Root vegetable pie

*Baked red cabbage;
Parsnip and potato
cakes*

BAKED RED CABBAGE

SERVES 4

350 g / 12 oz red cabbage, shredded
½ celery stick, chopped
50 g / 2 oz onion, sliced
1 small dessert apple, cored and diced
25 g / 1 oz raisins
250 ml / 8 fl oz cold water
1 tablespoon cider vinegar
⅛ teaspoon ground cinnamon
⅛ teaspoon ground coriander

Preparation time **10 minutes**
Cooking time **45 minutes**
Oven temperature **180 C, 350 F, gas 4**

1 Place one half of the cabbage in an ovenproof casserole dish and add the celery, onion, apple and raisins. Cover with the remaining cabbage. Mix together the water, vinegar and spices and pour on to the cabbage. Cover tightly and bake for 45 minutes. Serve at once.

Red cabbage makes a colourful accompaniment to many main courses. Although it is not such a good source of carotene – the plant form of vitamin A – as dark green cabbage, it contains many other valuable vitamins, minerals and fibre.

PARSNIP AND POTATO CAKES

SERVES 4

225 g / 8 oz potatoes
225 g / 8 oz parsnips
50 g / 2 oz onion, chopped
15 g / ½ oz butter or soft vegetable margarine
freshly ground black pepper
1 free-range egg
1 tablespoon sesame seeds
2 tablespoons wholemeal breadcrumbs
1–2 tablespoons oil
Garnish
tomato wedges
parsley sprigs

Preparation time **25 minutes, plus 15 minutes to chill**
Cooking time **30 minutes**

1 Peel the potatoes and parsnips and cut into 5-cm/2-in pieces. Place in a pan of cold water and bring to the boil. Reduce the heat and simmer for 15–20 minutes until soft. Drain.
2 While the vegetables are cooking, fry the onion lightly in the butter or margarine for 2 minutes. When the vegetables are cooked and drained, mash with the onion mixture. Do not make the mixture too soft or it will not hold its shape. Season with pepper and leave to cool.
3 Divide the mixture into four. Form each quarter into a burger shape. Beat the egg and pour into a shallow dish. In a second dish mix the sesame seeds and breadcrumbs together. Coat each burger first in the egg, then in the crumb mixture and shake off any excess. Place on a plate and chill in the refrigerator for 15 minutes.
4 Heat the oil in a frying pan and add the parsnip and potato cakes. Cook for 4 minutes on each side, until a deep golden colour. Remove and serve at once. Garnish with tomato wedges and parsley sprigs.

Shallow fry these parsnip and potato cakes in a very small amount of oil and heat up the oil before adding the cakes to the pan to quickly seal the outside of the food. This cuts down the amount of oil absorbed, keeping down the calorie and fat intake.

Baked red cabbage

Per portion:

Calories 50

Fat 0g

Fibre 4g

Freezing and Microwave note

Freeze after cooking by arranging each cake on a piece of foil and covering well. Defrost in the microwave on defrost setting for 4 minutes. Then heat through at full power for 3 minutes.

Parsnip and potato cakes

Per portion:

Calories 200

Fat 11g

Fibre 4g

CABBAGE AND SESAME STIR-FRY

SERVES 4

1 tablespoon sesame oil
100 g/4 oz onion, finely sliced
450 g/1 lb white cabbage, finely
shredded
2 tablespoons sesame seeds
freshly ground black pepper

Preparation time **5 minutes**
Cooking time **10 minutes**

1 Heat the oil in a wok or large heavy-based frying pan. Reserve a few onion rings for the garnish, then add the rest to the pan and cook for 1 minute.
2 Lower the heat slightly and stir in the shredded cabbage. Coat in the oil thoroughly and cook for about 4–5 minutes until the cabbage has lost its bite.
3 Stir in the sesame seeds, season with black pepper to taste, and transfer to one large serving dish or four individual dishes.
4 Serve immediately, garnished with the reserved onion rings.

Stir-frying is a technique used in Oriental cuisines to prepare vegetables or other ingredients quickly and with the minimum loss of nutrients.

This basic recipe shows you how to stir-fry, but there are numerous variations. You can pep up fresh vegetables, whether they are part of a Chinese meal or simply crisp, colourful accompaniments to many savoury dishes.

Variations
Vegetables such as cauliflower, broccoli, courgettes, celery, Chinese leaves, spinach, green cabbage, beanshoots can all be stir-fried successfully. The onion in the recipe can be replaced with 2–3 sliced spring onions or it can be omitted depending on the recipe.

The sesame flavour can be varied by using a lighter oil such as groundnut, soya or sunflower and omitting the sesame seeds. Vegetables such as cauliflower, courgettes and broccoli all require slightly longer cooking so they should be cut into fine florets or slices and added to the wok with a little stock and possibly a dash of soy sauce.

Cabbage and celery stir-fry: *use slightly less cabbage than the amount given in the main recipe and add a few finely sliced sticks of celery. Stir-fry the celery for a minute in sunflower oil, then add the cabbage and continue as above. Use the sesame seeds or add caraway seeds to flavour the dish.*

Cauliflower and courgette stir-fry: *break a medium cauliflower into tiny florets. Stir-fry in sunflower oil or flavour with walnut oil if you like. Add sliced courgettes and chopped spring onions and cook for a few minutes. Sprinkle with a few chopped walnuts before serving.*

Oriental-style stir-fry: *quickly stir-fry shredded Chinese leaves with shredded spring onions. Flavour the stir-fry with a little sesame oil if you like. Add beanshoots and broccoli florets and cook for a few minutes.*

Cauliflower and carrot stir-fry: *stir-fry carrot sticks and thinly sliced onion for a minute, then add cauliflower florets and stir-fry until almost cooked. Add a dash of soy sauce. Cook for a few minutes, then sprinkle in a little stock to moisten the stir-fry and heat through.*

Stir-fried beans with beanshoots: *stir-fry trimmed French beans with thinly sliced onion and a crushed clove of garlic. When just tender add beanshoots and cook for a few seconds. Sprinkle with parsley before serving.*

Cabbage and sesame stir-fry

Per portion:

Calories 110

Fat 7g

Fibre 4g

Cabbage and sesame stir-fry

Ritzy rice salad

Per portion:	
Calories 400	
Fat 15g	
Fibre 6g	

Waldorf salad

Per portion:	
Calories 160	
Fat 9g	
Fibre 3g	

RITZY RICE SALAD

SERVES 4

225 g/8 oz long-grain brown rice
225 g/8 oz carrots, scrubbed and finely grated
100 g/4 oz sunflower seeds
1 tablespoon mayonnaise
2 tablespoons chives, chopped
freshly ground black pepper

*Preparation time **10 minutes plus 30 minutes to chill***
*Cooking time **30 minutes***

1 Place the rice in a saucepan and cover with 2.5 cm/1 in of cold water. Bring to the boil, then simmer for 20–30 minutes until the rice is just tender. Drain.
2 Mix the cooked rice with the carrots, sunflower seeds and the mayonnaise.
3 Leave to chill for 30 minutes before stirring in the chopped chives. Season with black pepper to taste, and serve.

A healthy mixture of grains and seeds with lots of vitamin A (as carotene) in the carrots.

Variations
Rice salad is a versatile dish that can be served as an accompaniment for a main course or as a light meal, with some bread. Try some of the following variations that include other vegetables and nuts for flavour.
***Zesty rice salad:** a very easy way to vary the flavour – add the grated rind of 1 orange and mix in the juice squeezed from the fruit.*

***Ritzy rice with olives:** omit the carrots and use 175 g/6 oz roughly chopped tomatoes instead. Roughly chop 50 g/2 oz black olives and add to the salad. Serve with a bowl of freshly grated Parmesan cheese if you like.*

***Lemon rice with lentils:** instead of the carrots, add cooked green or red lentils to the rice. Flavour with the grated rind of 1 lemon and add some chopped spring onion.*

WALDORF SALAD

SERVES 4

4 celery sticks, chopped
50 g/2 oz walnuts, chopped
50 g/2 oz raisins
2 crisp dessert apples, cored and diced
1 tablespoon mayonnaise
1 tablespoon natural yogurt
freshly ground black pepper

*Preparation time **20 minutes***

1 Mix together the celery, walnuts, raisins and apples.
2 In a serving bowl, toss in the mayonnaise and yogurt and lightly season with pepper. Serve at once.

This crunchy classic salad makes a good side dish or, served on a bed of shredded lettuce, a light starter, full of fibre and low in calories.

Variations
Creamy, full-flavoured Waldorf salad can be turned into an interesting light meal by the addition of filling ingredients. Try the following ideas, serving warmed Granary bread or crusty wholemeal bread as an accompaniment.

***Pasta Waldorf:** mix 100–175 g/4–6 oz cooked wholemeal pasta shapes with the other salad ingredients. Add some extra chopped walnuts if you like.*

***Bean Waldorf:** drain 1 (425-g/15-oz) can red kidney beans and 1 (425-g/15-oz) can cannellini beans. Mix into the salad and sprinkle with some chopped fresh parsley.*

***Chick pea Waldorf:** add 2 (425-g/15-oz) cans chick-peas (drained) and flavour with a little crushed garlic if you like.*

Ritzy rice salad;
Waldorf salad

Honey raisin tart

Microwave note

**The flan case can be
baked blind in the
microwave on full
power for 4 minutes.
The filling can then be
added and decorated
as above and baked on
full power for another
4 minutes.**

Honey raisin tart

Per portion:

Calories 190

Fat 9g

Fibre 4g

HONEY RAISIN TART

SERVES 6

Pastry
100 g/4 oz plain wholemeal flour
50 g/2 oz soft vegetable margarine
cold water to mix
skimmed milk to glaze
Filling
75 g/3 oz wholemeal breadcrumbs
1 dessert apple, cored and grated
50 g/2 oz raisins
grated rind and juice of half a lemon
½ teaspoon ground cinnamon
2 tablespoons clear honey

Preparation time **25 minutes plus 15 minutes to chill**
Cooking time **25–30 minutes**
Oven temperature **200 C, 400 F, gas 6**
190 C, 375 F, gas 5

1 Place the flour in a bowl and rub in the margarine until the mixture resembles fine breadcrumbs. Chill for 10–15 minutes.
2 Add just enough water to the pastry mixture to bind to a dough. Roll out on a lightly floured surface and line a greased 18-cm/7-in flan dish or ring. Trim off and reserve any excess pastry. Bake blind for 10 minutes.
3 Meanwhile prepare the filling. Mix together the breadcrumbs with the grated apple, raisins, lemon rind, juice, cinnamon and honey. Spread in the baked flan case and decorate with any leftover pastry trimmings. Glaze the pastry with skimmed milk, reduce the heat of the oven and bake for 15–20 minutes until golden brown.

An unusual variation on the old-fashioned treacle tart. This tart, however, has extra fibre from the apple and raisins and is less sweet.

BAKED APPLES

SERVES 4

4 medium cooking apples (Bramleys are best)
75 g/3 oz ground almonds
25 g/1 oz wholemeal breadcrumbs
grated rind of ½ lemon
1 tablespoon orange juice
1 tablespoon clear honey
2 tablespoons cold water

Preparation time **10 minutes**
Cooking time **35–50 minutes**
Oven temperature **180 C, 350 F, gas 4**

1 Wipe the apples. Remove the core and make a slit around the middle of each apple.
2 Mix together the almonds, breadcrumbs, lemon rind, orange juice and honey, and use to fill the apple centres. Place the apples in a shallow ovenproof dish and place the cold water in the base of the dish. Bake for 35–50 minutes, depending on the size of the apples, until soft. Serve at once with yogurt.

Baked apples

Per portion:

Calories 120

Fat 10g

Fibre 4g

Microwave note
Bake the apples in the microwave on full power for 6–7 minutes; the exact time varies with size and variety of apple.

Baked apples

Orange and raisin cheesecake; Chestnut ice cream

ORANGE AND RAISIN CHEESECAKE

SERVES 6

Pastry
100 g/4 oz plain wholemeal flour
50 g/2 oz soft vegetable margarine
cold water to mix
Filling
2 free-range eggs, separated
2 tablespoons clear honey
225 g/8 oz low-fat soft cheese
juice of 1 orange
50 g/2 oz raisins

*Preparation time **30 minutes plus 15 minutes to chill***
*Cooking time **35–40 minutes***
*Oven temperature **200 C, 400 F, gas 6 180 C, 350 F, gas 4***

1 Place the flour in a bowl and rub in the margarine until the mixture resembles fine breadcrumbs. Chill for 10–15 minutes.
2 Add just enough water to the flour and margarine mixture to bind to a dough.
3 Roll out the pastry to line a 20-cm/ 8-in fluted flan ring. Bake blind for 10 minutes. Reduce oven temperature.
4 Beat the egg yolks with the honey until thick and pale. Beat in the cheese, orange juice and raisins.
5 Whisk the egg whites until stiff and gently fold them into the cheese mixture.
6 Pour the filling into the flan case and bake in the centre of the oven for 25–30 minutes, until golden brown and just firm to the touch.

The raisins and wholemeal pastry add fibre to this delicious cheesecake and the low-fat cheese helps to keep the calories down.

CHESTNUT ICE CREAM

SERVES 8

3 medium free-range eggs, separated
3 tablespoons clear honey
250 ml/8 fl oz skimmed milk
1 vanilla pod, split
400 g/14 oz chestnut purée
300 ml/½ pint natural yogurt

*Preparation time **45 minutes plus 20 minutes standing time and 4 hours to freeze***

1 Place the egg yolks with the honey in a large mixing bowl and whisk together until thick and creamy.
2 Heat the milk and vanilla pod slowly to boiling point. Remove from the heat and allow to stand until just warm. Beat into the egg mixture and then strain. Leave to cool completely.
3 Beat in the chestnut purée and yogurt.
4 Stiffly whisk the egg whites and gently fold into the mixture. Pour into a deep, rigid freezerproof container and freeze for about 4 hours until firm.
5 To serve, remove the ice cream from the freezer 30 minutes before serving, and keep in the refrigerator until ready to serve, in scoops.

A light, creamy ice cream; serve in scoops on its own or as a dessert accompaniment.

Orange and raisin cheesecake
Per portion:
Calories 210
Fat 9g
Fibre 2g

Chestnut ice cream
Per portion:
Calories 170
Fat 4g
Fibre 4g

CAROB REFRIGERATOR CRUNCH

MAKES 8 SLICES

225 g / 8 oz digestive biscuits, crushed
50 g / 2 oz raisins
50 g / 2 oz dried apricots, finely chopped
100 g / 4 oz soft vegetable margarine
2 tablespoons clear honey
75 g / 3 oz plain carob bar
Topping
25 g / 1 oz plain carob bar
2 generous tablespoons quark or other low-fat soft cheese

*Preparation time **25 minutes plus 1 hour to chill***
*Cooking time **5 minutes***

1 Mix the crushed digestive biscuits with the raisins and add the apricots.
2 Melt the margarine, honey and carob together and then stir in to the dry ingredients, mixing in thoroughly.
3 Press firmly into a greased 18-cm/7-in shallow cake tin and leave to chill in the refrigerator for 1 hour.
4 Make the topping by melting the carob and beating in the quark. Spread on top of the biscuit mixture and leave to set.

Carob is a popular alternative for those who are allergic to chocolate. It is also lower in sugar and is free from caffeine. This finger cake is a popular treat with children.

GINGERBREAD

MAKES 10 SLICES

100 g / 4 oz fine or medium oatmeal
175 g / 6 oz plain wholemeal flour
1 teaspoon bicarbonate of soda
1½ teaspoons ground ginger
½ teaspoon ground cinnamon
100 g / 4 oz sultanas
1 tablespoon honey
6 tablespoons molasses
75 g / 3 oz soft vegetable margarine
2 free-range eggs
150 ml / ¼ pint skimmed milk

*Preparation time **15 minutes***
*Cooking time **55–65 minutes***
*Oven temperature **160 C, 325 F, gas 3***

1 Place the oatmeal in a mixing bowl and sift in the flour, bicarbonate of soda, ginger and cinnamon. Stir in the sultanas.
2 Place the honey, molasses and margarine in a saucepan and heat gently until the margarine has melted.
3 Beat the eggs with the milk and add to the dry ingredients with the molasses mixture. Beat in thoroughly and pour into a greased and lined 20-cm/8-in shallow cake tin.
4 Bake for 50–60 minutes until the gingerbread is firm to the touch. Cool in the tin, then wrap in foil and store in an airtight tin.

Molasses is an excellent source of iron, and a healthier sweetener than sugar. The oats and wholemeal flour help to add fibre. The gingerbread tastes good cut into slices and spread with a little unsalted butter or vegetable margarine.

Carob refrigerator crunch

Per portion:

Calories 320

Fat 18g

Fibre 3g

Gingerbread

Per portion:

Calories 180

Fat 3g

Fibre 3g

Gingerbread; Carob refrigerator crunch

WINTER

DECEMBER · JANUARY · FEBRUARY

It may be cold outside but there is a huge array of fresh fruits and vegetables in store to liven up wintry days. Cabbages are plentiful – there are red, white and green to choose from. Brussels sprouts are also good value, as are broccoli and cauliflowers. Carrots, swedes, turnips, parsnips and leeks are cheap and plentiful and imported supplies of celery, sweet potatoes and fennel are available too.

Oranges, grapefruits, lemons and other imported fruits, including the more exotic figs and dates, boost home-grown apples and pears.

WINTER MENUS

Winter salad bowl with hot garlic bread

Almond roast with savoury baked potatoes and broccoli or Brussels sprouts

Fruit compote with Greek-style strained yogurt

Walnut-stuffed mushrooms

Winter bean pot with baked potato and lightly cooked cabbage

Fresh fruit salad and yogurt

Brussels soup

Oaty-topped root pie

Apple and orange charlotte

MINESTRONE SOUP

SERVES 4

2 tablespoons olive oil
100 g/4 oz onion, chopped
2 cloves garlic, crushed
225 g/8 oz carrot, scrubbed and diced
225 g/8 oz parsnip or swede, peeled and diced
100 g/4 oz potato, diced
100 g/4 oz pinto beans, soaked overnight
1 (425-g/15-oz) can tomatoes
1 tablespoon tomato purée
½ teaspoon marjoram or oregano
2 bay leaves
750 ml/1¼ pints vegetable stock
50 g/2 oz white cabbage
50 g/2 oz wholemeal pasta shapes
freshly ground black pepper
Garnish
grated Parmesan cheese
finely chopped parsley

*Preparation time **20 minutes, plus overnight soaking***
*Cooking time **1 hour 35 minutes***

1 Heat the oil in a large saucepan and stir in the onion, garlic and carrot. Cook gently for 2 minutes. Stir in the parsnip or swede and the potato and cook for a further minute.
2 Add the drained pinto beans, tomatoes, tomato purée, marjoram or oregano, bay leaves and stock and bring to the boil. Cover and simmer for 1¼ hours.
3 Shred the white cabbage finely and stir into the soup with the wholemeal pasta. Cook for 15 minutes or until the pasta is tender. Season with black pepper to taste and serve, garnished with Parmesan and parsley.

Adding some wholemeal pasta to the soup just before serving balances the protein in the beans.

BRUSSELS SOUP

SERVES 4

225 g/8 oz leeks
1 tablespoon sunflower oil
1 celery stick, chopped
225 g/8 oz Brussels sprouts, trimmed and chopped
½ teaspoon dried thyme
1 bay leaf
1 litre/1¾ pints vegetable stock
100 g/4 oz green split peas, soaked overnight
150 ml/¼ pint skimmed milk
freshly ground black pepper

*Preparation time **10 minutes, plus overnight soaking***
*Cooking time **45 minutes***

Minestrone soup

Per portion:	
Calories 320	
Fat 12g	
Fibre 15g	

Freezing note
This soup is best frozen at stage 2, after it has been cooked for 1¼ hours, but before the pasta and cabbage are added. Freeze in thick polythene bags or in an airtight container, then defrost at room temperature, or in the microwave for 15 minutes. Add the pasta and cabbage and turn to full power for a further 10 minutes.

Microwave note
Place the oil, leeks and celery in a large casserole dish, cover and cook on maximum power for 2 minutes. Stir in the sprouts and continue to cook for 2 further minutes. Add the split peas, stock and herbs and cook for 20 minutes, stirring after 10 minutes. Proceed with stage 4.

*Minestrone soup;
Brussels soup*

1 Trim the roots and coarse top leaves from the leeks. Shred, and wash thoroughly.

2 Heat the oil and stir in the leeks and celery. Cook gently for 2 minutes, covered. Stir in the sprouts and cook for a further minute.

3 Add the thyme, bay leaf and vegetable stock plus the drained split peas. Bring to the boil, cover and simmer for 40 minutes or until the split peas are quite soft.

4 Discard the bay leaf. Blend in a liquidiser to a smooth purée and reheat, stirring in the skimmed milk and seasoning to taste with black pepper. Wholemeal croûtons give texture, if preferred.

The addition of Brussels sprouts to this winter soup gives a rich colour and flavour. Split peas, like lentils, can be cooked successfully in the microwave to save time; larger pulses cook less well.

Brussels soup

Per portion:

Calories 150

Fat 4g

Fibre 8g

*Parsnip and potato
soup; Spiced lentil soup*

PARSNIP AND POTATO SOUP

SERVES 4

1 tablespoon sunflower oil
1 large onion, chopped
225 g/8 oz parsnips, chopped
350 g/12 oz potatoes, scrubbed and diced
150 ml/¼ pint skimmed milk
750 ml/1¼ pints vegetable stock
2 bay leaves
¼ teaspoon dried or ½ teaspoon chopped fresh thyme
freshly ground black pepper
natural yogurt to garnish

Preparation time **15 minutes**
Cooking time **50 minutes**

1 Heat the oil in a large saucepan and add the vegetables. Cook over a low heat for 2 minutes before adding the milk, stock, bay leaves and thyme. Cover, bring to the boil then simmer for 45 minutes until quite tender, remove bay leaves.
2 Blend the soup in a liquidiser to a smooth purée and season with black pepper to taste.
3 Reheat, then serve garnished with a swirl of yogurt.

A filling soup using readily available root vegetables.

SPICED LENTIL SOUP

SERVES 4

1 tablespoon sunflower oil
100 g/4 oz onion, chopped and 1 tablespoon reserved
1 clove garlic, crushed
1 celery stick, finely chopped
175 g/6 oz carrots, scrubbed and finely diced
½ teaspoon turmeric
¾ teaspoon ground cumin
pinch cayenne
175 g/6 oz red lentils
2 red peppers, deseeded and chopped
1.15 litres/2 pints vegetable stock
freshly ground black pepper
15 g/½ oz unsalted butter

Preparation time **15 minutes**
Cooking time **55 minutes**

1 Heat the oil in a large saucepan and add the prepared vegetables. Cook gently for 2 minutes then stir in the spices and cook for 1 further minute.
2 Stir in the red lentils, chopped pepper and stock. Bring to the boil, cover, reduce heat and simmer for 45 minutes.
3 Blend the soup in a liquidiser to a smooth purée and reheat, seasoning with black pepper to taste.
4 Melt the butter in a saucepan and stir in the reserved onion. Cook until rich and golden in colour. Serve soup in bowls, garnished with the fried onion.

A rich, warming soup with plenty of protein and fibre.

Spiced lentil soup

Per portion:

Calories 210

Fat 7g

Fibre 7g

Parsnip and potato soup

Per portion:

Calories 100

Fat 4g

Fibre 2g

CHEESY BAKED EGGS

SERVES 4

4 large free-range eggs
50 g/2 oz cheese, grated
freshly ground black pepper
1 tablespoon chopped parsley to
garnish

Preparation time **5 minutes**
Cooking time **7 minutes**
Oven temperature **180 C, 350 F, gas 4**

1 Lightly butter four ramekin dishes. Break the eggs into the dishes. Sprinkle the cheese on top of the eggs, with pepper to season.
2 Place the ramekins in a dish half-filled with water and bake for 6–7 minutes or until the whites of the eggs are just firm. Garnish with parsley and serve at once with wholemeal bread.

Cheddar cheese works well in this recipe, but a small amount of blue cheese adds a tangy, rich flavour.

Variations
Stilton eggs: a small amount of Stilton cheese, crumbled on top of the eggs in place of Cheddar gives a lovely rich flavour and colour and is a useful way of using up leftover Stilton from the Christmas holiday.

Mushroom eggs: place a little finely sliced mushroom in the base of the lightly buttered ramekins and proceed as detailed.

Peppered eggs: place some finely chopped red or green pepper in the base of the lightly buttered ramekins and proceed as detailed. Leave out the parsley and garnish instead with a sprinkling of cayenne.

Soft baked eggs: omit the Cheddar cheese from the recipe and top the eggs instead with 2 teaspoons of low-fat soft cheese, mixed with some finely chopped chives, garlic and parsley.

Spinach eggs: place a little cooked, chopped spinach in the base of each ramekin and proceed as detailed. Season with a little freshly grated nutmeg.

Baked eggs with vegetables: place a mixture of diced, cooked root vegetables in the base of a large ovenproof dish. For example, mix some potato, carrot, swede, parsnip and celeriac. Make four neat spaces for the eggs. Crack an egg into each hollow and bake as in the main recipe, allowing a few minutes extra, to heat the vegetables and set the eggs.

Baked eggs with courgettes: roughly chop and blanch 4 courgettes. Place in an ovenproof dish, then sprinkle with chopped parsley and make four holes for the eggs. Sprinkle with chopped parsley and a little crumbled Stilton cheese, then bake as above, allowing extra cooking time for the courgettes.

Baked eggs with rice: a good way of turning leftover cooked rice into a tasty supper. Place cooked long-grain brown rice in an ovenproof dish, making four holes for the eggs. Crack an egg into each space and sprinkle with a little grated Parmesan or Cheddar cheese. Bake until set, then add some chopped chives before serving.

Microwave note
This recipe can be prepared in the microwave. The yolk of the egg must be pierced before sprinkling the cheese on top. Cook on half power for 1$\frac{1}{2}$–1$\frac{3}{4}$ minutes.

Cheesy baked eggs

Per portion:
Calories 140
Fat 10g
Fibre 0g

Soft baked eggs

Per portion:
Calories 110
Fat 6g
Fibre 0g

Cheesy baked eggs

HOT COLESLAW

SERVES 4

225 g/8 oz white cabbage, finely shredded
100 g/4 oz red cabbage, finely shredded
100 g/4 oz carrots, grated
1 red-skinned dessert apple, cored and finely diced
2 teaspoons lemon juice
1 tablespoon grated onion
2 tablespoons skimmed milk
2 free-range egg yolks
generous pinch mustard powder
1 teaspoon clear honey
1 tablespoon sunflower oil
4 tablespoons cider vinegar
freshly ground black pepper
2 tablespoons natural yogurt

*Preparation time **15 minutes***
*Cooking time **5 minutes***

1 Mix together the white and red cabbage with the carrots in a mixing bowl.
2 Toss the diced apple in the lemon juice and add to the cabbage mixture. Mix in the grated onion.
3 Blend the milk, egg yolks, mustard, honey, oil and vinegar with some black pepper in a liquidiser until smooth.
4 Heat the mixture over a pan of hot water to thicken and beat in the yogurt.
5 Pour the dressing over the cabbage mixture and toss thoroughly together. Serve at once with warmed bread.

A hot dressing transforms coleslaw into a warming starter for colder days.

Hot coleslaw

Per portion:

Calories 130

Fat 7g

Fibre 3g

CHICK-PEA PÂTÉ

SERVES 4

100 g/4 oz chick-peas, soaked
overnight
2 cloves garlic
3 tablespoons tahini
pinch paprika
½ teaspoon ground cumin
3–5 tablespoons cold water
juice of half a lemon
freshly ground black pepper

Preparation time **15 minutes plus**
overnight soaking
Cooking time **2 hours (or 20 minutes)**

1 Drain the chick-peas and put in a saucepan. Add plenty of boiling water to cover the pulses by about 5 cm/2 in. Cover and boil for 2 hours or until tender. Alternatively pressure cook at 15-lb pressure for 20 minutes. Drain.
2 Place the chick-peas in a liquidiser with the remaining ingredients and blend to a purée or mash. Add some extra water for a fairly smooth texture, if necessary.
3 Serve the pâté with wholemeal toast or with vegetable crudités.

This pâté is a good source of protein, because of the combination of the chick-peas and the tahini. It has a rich flavour and a good texture. Any that is left over could be used as a tasty sandwich filling; simply add some shredded lettuce or sliced cucumber.
Tahini is a pale, slightly oily, paste made from sesame seeds. It is available from health food shops.

Chick-pea pâté

Per portion:

Calories 140

Fat 8g

Fibre 5g

Hot coleslaw; Chick-pea
pâté

125

ALMOND ROAST

SERVES 6

225 g / 8 oz button mushrooms
175 g / 6 oz carrot, scrubbed and grated
1 onion, chopped
1 celery stick, diced
225 g / 8 oz ground almonds
225 g / 8 oz wholemeal breadcrumbs
1 tablespoon finely grated lemon rind
1 teaspoon chopped fresh or ½ teaspoon dried thyme
1 tablespoon chopped parsley
3 free-range eggs
freshly ground black pepper

Preparation time **20 minutes**
Cooking time **45 minutes**
Oven temperature **190 C, 375 F, gas 5**

1 Line and lightly oil a 20-cm/8-in ring tin or 450-g/1-lb loaf tin. If using the loaf tin, the quantities should be halved.
2 Wipe the mushrooms and chop very finely. Place all the vegetables in a mixing bowl.
3 Stir in the almonds, breadcrumbs, lemon rind, thyme and parsley. Mix in thoroughly.
4 Beat the eggs together and mix into the dry ingredients, adding a little water to bind the mixture together. Season with pepper and place in the prepared tin. Smooth the top, cover with foil and bake for 35 minutes. Remove the foil and continue cooking for a further 10 minutes. Serve hot or leave to cool thoroughly before serving sliced, cold. A festive presentation is shown below.

If using the ring tin, serve lightly boiled Brussels sprouts in the centre.

Variations
Nut roasts: *Any nuts can be used in place of almonds: cashews, hazelnuts, peanuts, walnuts, brazils and pecans all make tasty nut roasts although the latter three do impart a stronger flavour.*
Tofu and almond roast: *Make a vegan, dairy-free roast by omitting the eggs and binding the mixture instead with 225 g / 8 oz tofu, adding a little vegetable stock if necessary, and some extra herbs of your choice to the basic mixture.*

Carrot and tomato nut roast: *Omit the mushrooms and use 275 g / 10 oz sliced carrots plus 2 peeled and chopped tomatoes and 2 tablespoons tomato purée (this works well with walnuts or brazils).*

WALNUT-STUFFED MUSHROOMS

SERVES 4

1 tablespoon olive oil
8 large open mushrooms
50 g / 2 oz onion, chopped
1 clove garlic, crushed
75 g / 3 oz walnuts, ground or chopped
50 g / 2 oz wholemeal breadcrumbs
1 teaspoon chopped fresh or ½ teaspoon rubbed sage
1 free-range egg
1 tablespoon tomato purée
freshly ground black pepper
50 g / 2 oz double Gloucester cheese, grated
chopped parsley to garnish

Preparation time **15 minutes**
Cooking time **25 minutes**
Oven temperature **200 C, 400 F, gas 6**

1 Lightly oil a shallow ovenproof dish.
2 Wipe the mushrooms and remove the stalks. Place the mushrooms in the dish.
3 Cook the onion and garlic lightly in the oil for 2 minutes.
4 Mix the walnuts with the onion and garlic, breadcrumbs and sage. Bind with the egg and tomato purée and season with pepper. Stuff the mixture into the mushrooms and press into the base. Sprinkle the cheese on top. Bake for 20 minutes. Garnish with parsley and serve hot.

A fibre-rich and attractive first course.

Variations
Parmesan-stuffed mushrooms: *Replace the Double Gloucester cheese with 4 tablespoons Parmesan cheese, to give the mixture a rich flavour. Parmesan works best with a herb like oregano or marjoram so use one of these instead of sage.*

Microwave note
Cook the Walnut-stuffed mushrooms in the microwave on full power for 4 minutes, then finish off under a hot grill to just brown the top.

Almond roast

Per portion:

Calories 350

Fat 25g

Fibre 10g

Walnut-stuffed mushrooms

Per portion:

Calories 250

Fat 20g

Fibre 3g

Almond roast; Walnut-stuffed mushrooms

Sesame-walnut mushrooms: Use a tablespoon of sunflower or sesame seeds in place of $7g/\frac{1}{4}oz$ of the nuts to add extra flavour and texture.

Courgette-stuffed mushrooms: trim and grate I large courgette, then mix into the stuffing instead of the nuts.

Leek and cashew mushrooms: trim and finely chop I small leek, then cook in I tablespoon sunflower oil for about 2 minutes, to soften. Mix with the stuffing, substituting chopped cashew nuts for the walnuts. Flavour with chopped parsley instead of the sage.

Tomato-stuffed mushrooms: peel and finely chop 2 tomatoes and mix into the stuffing with $25g/$ I oz chopped peanuts instead of the walnuts. Proceed as in the main recipe. A pinch of chopped thyme is a good flavouring ingredient for this variation.

Winter lasagne

Per portion:

Calories 400

Fat 12g

Fibre 4g

Chick-pea crumble

Per portion:

Calories 500

Fat 25g

Fibre 12g

WINTER LASAGNE

SERVES 4

1 tablespoon sunflower oil
100 g/4 oz onion, finely chopped
1 clove garlic, crushed
100 g/4 oz carrot, scrubbed and diced
100 g/4 oz potato, scrubbed and diced
75 g/3 oz mushrooms, sliced
1 small green pepper, deseeded and chopped
1 (425-g/15-oz) can tomatoes
75 g/3 oz continental lentils
150 ml/¼ pint vegetable stock
1 bay leaf
¼ teaspoon marjoram
300 ml/½ pint water
10 pieces of no pre-cook wholewheat lasagne
3 free-range eggs
300 ml/½ pint natural yogurt
freshly ground black pepper
50 g/2 oz Cheddar cheese, finely grated

*Preparation time **20 minutes***
*Cooking time **1 hour 25 minutes***
*Oven temperature **190 C, 375 F, gas 5***

1 To make the lentil sauce. Heat the oil in a saucepan and gently cook the onion, garlic, carrot and potato for 3 minutes. Stir in the mushrooms, pepper, tomatoes, lentils, stock and herbs. Bring the sauce to the boil, reduce the heat and simmer for 40 minutes, stirring from time to time.
2 When the lentil mixture is cooked stir in the 300 ml/½ pint water.
3 Spread one-third of the lasagne sauce in the base of an oiled, oblong ovenproof dish and top with one-third of the lasagne. Add two more layers of sauce and lasagne, finishing with the lasagne.
4 Beat the eggs with the yogurt and season well with black pepper.
5 Pour over the top of the lasagne and sprinkle with the cheese. Bake in the oven for 40 minutes until browned on top.

A filling dish which is very flavoursome and has plenty of protein and fibre.

CHICK-PEA CRUMBLE

SERVES 4

1 tablespoon sunflower oil
100 g/4 oz onion, finely chopped
1 celery stick, finely sliced
225 g/8 oz potatoes, scrubbed and sliced
1 (425-g/15-oz) can tomatoes
½ teaspoon ground cumin
¼ teaspoon basil or marjoram
1 (425-g/15-oz) can chick-peas or 175 g/6 oz dried chick-peas, cooked
freshly ground black pepper
Crumble
75 g/3 oz plain wholemeal flour
25 g/1 oz rolled oats
50 g/2 oz soft vegetable margarine
1 tablespoon sunflower seeds
2 tablespoons sesame seeds

*Preparation time **15 minutes***
*Cooking time **50 minutes***
*Oven temperature **190 C, 375 F, gas 5***

1 Heat the oil in a large saucepan and add the onion, celery and potatoes. Cook gently for 2 minutes. Stir in the tomatoes, breaking them up with the back of a spoon. Add the cumin and basil and bring to the boil. Reduce the heat and simmer gently for 20 minutes.
2 Stir in the chick-peas, season with black pepper to taste and set aside.
3 Make the crumble by placing the flour and oats in a mixing bowl. Rub in the margarine until the mixture resembles fine breadcrumbs.
4 Lightly toast the seeds either under a hot grill or in a dry, heavy-based frying pan. Add to the crumble mixture.
5 Pour the chick-pea sauce into the base of a greased ovenproof dish and sprinkle over the crumble mixture.
6 Bake in the centre of the oven for 20 minutes until golden brown. Serve hot.

A warming, nutritious dish with plenty of protein for chilly winter evenings.

Winter lasagne; Chick-pea crumble

WINTER BEAN POT

SERVES 4

*2 leeks, trimmed and washed
1 tablespoon sunflower oil
100g/4oz onion, chopped
2 cloves garlic, crushed
225g/8oz carrots, scrubbed and diced
225g/8oz parsnip, peeled and diced
100g/4oz turnip, peeled and diced
1 (425-g/15-oz) can tomatoes
1 tablespoon tomato purée
1.25 litres/2¼ pints vegetable stock
1 bay leaf
½ teaspoon dried basil or oregano
2 tablespoons pot barley
100g/4oz butter beans, soaked
overnight
75g/3oz pinto beans, soaked overnight
freshly ground black pepper*

*Preparation time **10 minutes, plus
overnight soaking**
Cooking time **1 hour 20 minutes**
Oven temperature **190C, 375F, gas 5***

1 Slice the leeks into 1-cm/½-in rings.
2 Heat the oil in a large saucepan or in the base of a flameproof casserole. Cook the onion, garlic and leeks for 2 minutes. Then stir in the carrots, parsnip and turnip and cook for 1 minute.
3 Add the tomatoes and tomato purée and stir in thoroughly. Add the stock, bay leaf, basil or oregano, pot barley and drained beans. Mix in well, bring to the boil, then bake for 1–1¼ hours or until the beans are tender. Season and serve.

Warming dishes like this one are perfect for cold winter evenings. Serve with jacket potatoes topped with grated cheese.

Winter bean pot

Per portion:

Calories 240

Fat 4g

Fibre 15g

Winter bean pot;
Potato layer bake

POTATO LAYER BAKE

SERVES 4

100 g / 4 oz onion, sliced
675 g / 1½ lb potatoes, peeled and sliced
1 clove garlic, crushed (optional)
freshly ground black pepper
75 g / 3 oz farmhouse Cheddar cheese,
finely grated
skimmed milk
chopped parsley to garnish

Preparation time **10 minutes**
Cooking time **1¼–1½ hours**
Oven temperature **180 C, 350 F, gas 4**

1 Lightly oil a shallow ovenproof dish.
2 Arrange the onion and potato slices in layers with the garlic, if using. Season with pepper and scatter the Cheddar on top. Pour over sufficient skimmed milk to come almost to the top of the potatoes, and bake for 1¼–1½ hours until tender. Garnish with freshly chopped parsley.

This method of cooking potatoes makes a superb side dish for more formal meals. If preferred, a little crushed garlic can be added to give extra flavour.

Potato layer bake	
Per portion:	
Calories 220	
Fat 6g	
Fibre 4g	

Hot pot with dumplings; Baked cauliflower

HOT POT WITH DUMPLINGS

SERVES 4

100 g/4 oz onion, chopped
1 celery stick, sliced
225 g/8 oz swede, diced
225 g/8 oz carrots, sliced into rings
225 g/8 oz potato, diced
100 g/4 oz pot barley
50 g/2 oz red kidney beans, soaked overnight
1 litre/1¾ pints vegetable stock
½ teaspoon dried thyme
pinch dried rosemary
1 tablespoon tomato purée
Dumplings
100 g/4 oz plain wholemeal flour
50 g/2 oz soft vegetable margarine
pinch dried rosemary
freshly ground black pepper
water to mix

Preparation time **20 minutes plus overnight soaking**
Cooking time **2 hours 20 minutes**

1 Place the onion, celery, swede, carrots, potato, pot barley and drained kidney beans in a large saucepan and add the stock, herbs, and tomato purée. Bring to the boil and keep boiling for 10 minutes, then reduce heat and simmer for 1¾ hours.
2 Meanwhile make the dumplings: put the margarine in the freezer or freezing compartment of the refrigerator until very firm. Place the flour in a bowl, grate the margarine and stir in with the rosemary and the black pepper. Add just enough cold water to mix to a moist dough.
3 Shape into dumplings and add to the pan, cook with the lid on for 20 minutes. Serve the hot pot at once with Brussels sprouts or other fresh green vegetables.

Pot or Scotch barley is more nutritious than pearl barley as it contains more fibre and B vitamins. It makes a tasty addition to soups and casseroles and the dumplings add extra sustenance.

BAKED CAULIFLOWER

SERVES 4

1 large cauliflower divided into florets
1 bay leaf
1 tablespoon sunflower oil
100 g/4 oz onion, finely chopped
4 free-range eggs
150 ml/¼ pint milk
2 tablespoons chopped parsley
freshly ground black pepper
25 g/1 oz Cheddar cheese, grated

Preparation time **15 minutes**
Cooking time **40 minutes**
Oven temperature **200 C, 400 F, gas 6**

1 Place the cauliflower florets in pan with a small amount of boiling water in it. Add the bay leaf and boil for 6–8 minutes, until tender. Drain and reserve.
2 Heat the oil in a saucepan and cook the onion for 2 minutes over a low heat without browning.
3 Arrange the cauliflower in a 23-cm/9-in pie plate and sprinkle the onion on top.
4 Beat the eggs with the milk and parsley and season with black pepper to taste. Pour over the cauliflower and top with grated cheese.
5 Bake in the centre of the oven for 30 minutes, until golden brown and well risen. Serve at once with baked potatoes.

An easily prepared dish which is very well balanced in protein. The dish could also be varied by using broccoli or leeks in place of the cauliflower.

Hot pot with dumplings

Per portion:
Calories 370
Fat 12g
Fibre 12g

Baked cauliflower

Per portion:
Calories 180
Fat 12g
Fibre 3g

*Aduki and pepper
quiche; Oaty-topped
root pie*

**Aduki and pepper
quiche**

Per portion:
Calories 330
Fat 19g
Fibre 6g

Microwave note
**The flan case can be
baked blind in the
microwave for 4
minutes on full power
if preferred. Proceed as
recipe. The quiche can
also be reheated in the
microwave on medium
power for 5 minutes.**

ADUKI AND PEPPER QUICHE

SERVES 4

Pastry
100 g | 4 oz plain wholemeal flour
50 g | 2 oz soft vegetable margarine
cold water to mix
Filling
50 g | 2 oz aduki beans, soaked overnight
1 small onion, chopped
1 tablespoon oil
50 g | 2 oz button mushrooms
½ green pepper, chopped
2 free-range eggs
150 ml | ¼ pint natural yogurt
freshly ground black pepper
25 g | 1 oz Cheddar cheese, grated
curly endive to garnish

Preparation time **20 minutes, plus
overnight soaking and 15 minutes to
chill**
Cooking time **45 minutes**
Oven temperature **200 C, 400 F, gas 6**

1 Cook the aduki beans for 45–50 minutes, or 12 minutes at 6.75 kg/15 lb pressure in a pressure cooker and drain.
2 Sift the flour into a mixing bowl and add the bran from the sieve. Rub in the margarine until the mixture resembles fine breadcrumbs. Place the bowl in the refrigerator to rest for 15 minutes.
3 Cook the onion gently for 2 minutes in the oil. Stir in the mushrooms and pepper and cook for a further minute. Mix in the aduki beans and remove from the heat.
4 Add enough cold water to the flour and margarine mixture to mix to a soft dough. Roll out on a lightly floured work surface, then use to line an 18-cm/7-in flan ring or dish. Bake blind for 10 minutes.
5 Place the bean mixture in the flan case. In a bowl, beat together the eggs, yogurt and black pepper. Pour the mixture over the filling. Sprinkle the cheese on top. Return to the oven for 25–30 minutes until the filling is set. Serve hot or cold, garnished with curly endive.

This substantial quiche is equally good served hot or cold. The beans add extra protein and fibre. Serve with a salad and wholemeal bread or a baked potato.

OATY-TOPPED ROOT PIE

SERVES 6

Pastry
175g/6oz plain wholemeal flour
50g/2oz rolled oats
100g/4oz soft vegetable margarine
cold water to mix
skimmed milk to glaze

Filling
40g/1½oz soft vegetable margarine
2 leeks, trimmed, washed and chopped
2 celery sticks, chopped
275g/10oz carrots, scrubbed and diced
275g/10oz parsnips, peeled and diced
3 tablespoons plain wholemeal flour
450ml/¾ pint vegetable stock

Preparation time **35 minutes, plus time to chill**
Cooking time **35 minutes**
Oven temperature **200 C, 400 F, gas 6**

1 Place the flour and oats in a mixing bowl, reserving 1 tablespoon oats, and rub in the margarine, until the mixture resembles fine breadcrumbs. Place in the refrigerator to rest while preparing the filling.

2 Melt the margarine in a pan and add the vegetables. Cook gently for 3 minutes. Stir in the flour and cook for 2 minutes. Gradually add the stock, stirring well to make a smooth sauce. Simmer for 10 minutes, stirring occasionally to prevent sticking. Remove from the heat and pour into a deep 900-ml/1½-pint pie dish.

3 Add just enough water to the pastry mixture to make a soft dough. Roll out on a lightly floured surface to a size slightly larger than the top of the pie dish. Cut a narrow strip of pastry from the edge and use to line the dampened rim of the pie dish. Brush with water, then top with the pastry lid. Trim edges, flute and glaze with milk. Sprinkle over the reserved oats. Bake for 30 minutes.

Oats are a good source of a particular type of fibre which is known to help lower the level of cholesterol in the blood. One good way to increase the quantity of oats in the diet is to substitute oats for 25g/ 1oz wholemeal flour in a basic pastry mixture using 100g/4oz flour.

Oaty-topped root pie	
Per portion:	
Calories 360	
Fat 20g	
Fibre 8g	

Microwave note
At stage 2, place the margarine and vegetables in a covered dish and cook on maximum power for 5 minutes. Add the flour and stock and return to cook for a further 5 minutes. Place in the pie dish and proceed with stage 3.

Sunflower tartlets

Per tartlet:

Calories 130

Fat 8g

Fibre 2g

Leek quiche

Per portion:

Calories 280

Fat 18g

Fibre 2g

SUNFLOWER TARTLETS

MAKES 12

Pastry
100 g/4 oz plain wholemeal flour
50 g/2 oz soft vegetable margarine
cold water to mix
Filling
2 teaspoons sunflower oil
50 g/2 oz onion, finely chopped
½ green pepper, deseeded and chopped
4 tablespoons sweetcorn kernels
1 free-range egg
3 tablespoons skimmed milk
freshly ground black pepper
40 g/1½ oz Cheddar cheese, finely grated
3 tablespoons sunflower seeds
Garnish
1 tomato
watercress sprigs

Preparation time **25 minutes plus 15 minutes to chill**
Cooking time **20 minutes**
Oven temperature **200 C, 400 F, gas 6**

---

1 Place flour in bowl and rub in the margarine until mixture resembles fine breadcrumbs. Chill for 10–15 minutes and then add just enough water to make a soft dough. Roll out the dough to a rectangle and cut out rounds with a pastry cutter to line 12 greased patty tins.
2 Carefully press the pastry into the tins and bake blind for 5 minutes.
3 Prepare the filling. Heat the oil in a saucepan and cook the onion and pepper for a few minutes over a low heat. Stir in the sweetcorn kernels and continue to cook for 2 minutes.
4 Beat the egg with the milk and season with black pepper to taste.
5 Divide the onion mixture between the tarts, spoon a little egg and milk mixture over the top and sprinkle grated cheese and sunflower seeds on top. Bake for 10–12 minutes until the filling is set and golden brown.
6 Serve hot or cold, garnished with tomato and watercress.

LEEK QUICHE

SERVES 4

Pastry
100 g/4 oz plain wholemeal flour
50 g/2 oz soft vegetable margarine
cold water to mix
Filling
350 g/12 oz leeks, sliced into rings
2 free-range eggs
150 ml/¼ pint skimmed milk
sprig fresh rosemary, chopped or ¼ teaspoon dried rosemary
freshly ground black pepper
50 g/2 oz Red Leicester or Cheshire cheese, finely grated

Preparation time **25 minutes plus 15 minutes to chill**
Cooking time **45 minutes**
Oven temperature **200 C, 400 F, gas 6**
190 C, 375 F, gas 5

---

1 Place the flour in a bowl and rub in the margarine until mixture resembles fine breadcrumbs. Chill for 10–15 minutes, then add just enough water to make a soft dough.
2 Roll out and line a greased 18-cm/7-in flan ring or dish. Bake blind for 10 minutes and then reduce heat.
3 Reserve a few slices of leek for the garnish. Plunge the remainder into a small amount of boiling water and cook for 8 minutes until just tender. Drain and reserve.
4 Beat the eggs with the milk, rosemary and black pepper to taste.
5 Arrange the cooked leeks in the pastry case, pour over the egg mixture and sprinkle the cheese on the top.
6 Bake for 25 minutes until the filling is set and golden brown. Garnish with the reserved leek, separated into rings.

A light quiche, making good use of leeks. Ideal for lunch or supper.

Sunflower tartlets; Leek
quiche

CHEESY BAKED POTATOES

SERVES 4

*4 (225-g/8-oz) potatoes
100g/4oz onion, chopped
1 tablespoon sunflower oil
100g/4oz mushrooms, diced
100g/4oz farmhouse Cheddar cheese, grated
a little skimmed milk
freshly ground black pepper*
Garnish
*halved tomato slices
parsley sprigs
curly endive*

---

*Preparation time **12 minutes**
Cooking time **1 hour 40 minutes**
Oven temperature **200C, 400F, gas 6***

---

1 Scrub the potatoes and pierce the skins with a fork in six places. Bake for 1–1¼ hours until the insides are soft.
2 Cook the onion in the oil gently for 3 minutes and stir in the mushrooms; cook for 1 minute, then set aside.
3 When the potatoes are cooked, cut each one in half and scoop out the insides, retaining the skin. Mash the potato in a mixing bowl with the onion and mushroom mixture and half of the Cheddar, adding just enough milk to mix to a smooth texture. Season with pepper.
4 Arrange the potato shells in a shallow ovenproof dish and pile in the potato mixture. Sprinkle the remaining cheese on top and return to the oven for 20 minutes until the cheese has melted and is bubbling. Serve garnished as shown.

Baked potatoes make a good sustaining light meal when served with toppings such as cottage cheese, mushrooms and grated cheese, or make the perfect accompaniment to many main dishes when served with a little butter or margarine and lashings of black pepper. This recipe takes a little extra time to prepare, but the result is well worth the effort.

CHESTNUT PIE

SERVES 6

Filling
*225g/8oz chestnuts
2 celery sticks, chopped
175g/6oz onion, chopped
1 clove garlic, crushed
1 tablespoon sunflower oil
3 tablespoons chopped parsley
1 teaspoon dried or 2 teaspoons chopped fresh thyme
grated rind of ½ lemon
175g/6oz wholemeal breadcrumbs
2 free-range eggs
2–3 tablespoons vegetable stock
450g/1 lb Brussels sprouts
freshly ground black pepper
salad ingredients to garnish*
Pastry
*175g/6oz soft vegetable margarine
350g/12oz plain wholemeal flour
cold water to mix
beaten egg to glaze*

---

*Preparation time **50 minutes, plus 10 minutes to chill**
Cooking time **2 hours**
Oven temperature **200C, 400F, gas 6**
180C, 350F, gas 4*

---

1 Lightly oil a game pie mould, or oil a deep 15-cm/6-in round cake tin and line with greaseproof paper.
2 Prepare the chestnuts by slitting the shells and skins with a knife, bringing them to the boil in water and simmering for 3 minutes. Peel away the chestnut skins. Chop the chestnuts finely.
3 Cook the celery, onion and garlic together in the oil for a few minutes without browning. Stir into the chestnuts and add the parsley, thyme, lemon rind and breadcrumbs. Mix in thoroughly. Beat the eggs and add to the bowl with just enough stock to bind to a moist consistency. Garnish as shown.
4 Make the pastry. Rub the margarine into the flour until the mixture resembles fine breadcrumbs. Chill for 10 minutes.
5 Trim the sprouts and cook in boiling water for 15–20 minutes until really soft. Drain and mash or chop finely and season.
6 Add just enough cold water to the pastry to make a soft dough. Roll out two-

Baked potatoes cook quickly in the microwave but lack the crisp skin obtained by cooking in the conventional oven. This recipe, however, works really well in the microwave. Wrap the scrubbed and pierced potatoes separately in pieces of kitchen paper and place on full power in the microwave. Cook for 20 minutes. Unwrap and leave to stand for 5 minutes before proceeding as recipe. Return the filled potatoes to the microwave for 3 minutes until the cheese has melted.

Cheesy baked potatoes
Per portion:
Calories 340
Fat 12g
Fibre 5g

Chestnut pie
Per portion:
Calories 586
Fat 30g
Fibre 14g

Microwave note

Slit the chestnut shells and skins, rinse and place the nuts in a basin and cook on full power for 5 minutes. The skins will easily peel away. Brussels sprouts cook in around 8–10 minutes on full power in the microwave, if placed with a little water in a covered casserole dish.

Chestnut pie; Cheesy baked potatoes

thirds of the pastry to fit the base and sides of the pie mould or tin and line. Place one half of the chestnut mixture in the base, top with sprouts, then place the remaining chestnut mixture on top. Roll out the remaining pastry and place on top. Seal the edges and shape any pastry trimmings into leaves to decorate. Glaze with the beaten egg and bake for 20 minutes, then lower the oven temperature for a further 45 minutes. Leave in the pie mould or tin to cool, or serve hot.

A splendid winter pie which should be made in a raised pie mould for best results.

Lentil and potato pie

Per portion:

Calories 300

Fat 6g

Fibre 10g

LENTIL AND POTATO PIE

SERVES 4

1 tablespoon olive oil
100g/4oz onion, chopped
1 celery stick, chopped
2 cloves garlic, crushed
100g/4oz open mushrooms, chopped
1 (425-g/15-oz) can tomatoes
1 green or red pepper, deseeded and
chopped
1 tablespoon tomato purée
175g/6oz brown lentils
150ml/¼ pint vegetable stock
1 bay leaf
Topping
450g/1 lb potatoes
knob of unsalted butter
dash of skimmed milk

Preparation time **10 minutes**
Cooking time **1 hour 25 minutes**

1 Heat the oil and add the onion, celery and garlic. Cook gently for 2 minutes. Add the mushrooms, tomatoes, pepper, tomato purée, lentils, stock and bay leaf. Bring to the boil, cover and simmer for 1 hour until the lentils are quite soft.
2 Meanwhile, peel the potatoes and cut into 5-cm/2-in pieces and place in cold water. Bring to the boil, reduce the heat and simmer steadily for 15–20 minutes until soft. Drain and mash with butter and a dash of skimmed milk to a smooth consistency.
3 Heat the grill and warm a flameproof dish. Place the lentil mixture in the dish and top with the mashed potato. Grill for 5 minutes or until the top is crusty and brown. Serve with Brussels sprouts or a dark green leafy cabbage.

Brown lentils are a good source of protein, fibre, minerals and B vitamins and are much lower in fat than the conventional minced meat used in shepherd's pie. But they are surprisingly tasty too and non-vegetarians will be won over by this simple supper dish.

BAKED RICE

SERVES 4

225g/8oz long-grain brown rice
750ml/1¼ pints water
1 tablespoon tomato purée
½ teaspoon yeast extract
1 bay leaf
150g/5oz red lentils
175g/6oz carrots, scrubbed and sliced
175g/6oz sweet potato, scrubbed and
diced
100g/4oz swede or parsnip, peeled and
diced
100g/4oz onion, chopped
1 teaspoon cumin seeds
pinch of cayenne
½ teaspoon turmeric

Baked rice

Per portion:

Calories **400**

Fat **1g**

Fibre **11g**

Baked rice; Lentil and potato pie

Preparation time **10 minutes**
Cooking time **1 hour 10 minutes**
Oven temperature **200 C, 400 F, gas 6**
180 C, 350 F, gas 4

---

1 Place the rice in a large casserole dish with the water, tomato purée, yeast extract and bay leaf. Bake for 30 minutes.
2 Turn down the oven temperature. Stir in the lentils, prepared vegetables, cumin seeds, cayenne and turmeric. Bake for a further 40 minutes.
3 Transfer the baked rice to a serving dish and serve at once. Brussels sprouts make a good accompaniment.

An unusual method of cooking rice in the oven with red lentils and nutritious root vegetables, including the flavourful sweet potato, now widely available at this time of year. Despite the name, sweet pota-toes are not related to potatoes. Although first imported into Europe in the sixteenth century, this vegetable is not currently a popular ingredient in the English diet. But do experiment with it in this tasty dish.

Mushroom and almond pilaff; Spicy lentils with rice

MUSHROOM AND ALMOND PILAFF

SERVES 4

*1 tablespoon sunflower oil
pinch cumin seeds
1 clove garlic, chopped
75 g|3 oz onion, finely chopped
¼ teaspoon ground turmeric
225 g|8 oz long-grain brown rice
550 ml|18 fl oz water
175 g|6 oz button mushrooms, finely chopped
1 bay leaf
75 g|3 oz split almonds, lightly toasted
freshly ground black pepper
a few whole almonds for garnish*

Preparation time **10 minutes**
Cooking time **35 minutes**

---

1 Heat the oil in a saucepan and add the cumin seeds. Let them sizzle for 15 seconds then stir in the garlic and onion and cook over a low heat for 2 minutes. Stir in the turmeric and cook for 1 minute.
2 Stir in the rice and cook for 1 minute to let the grains turn transparent.
3 Stir in the water, mushrooms, bay leaf and bring to the boil. Cover, reduce heat and simmer for 25–30 minutes until the rice is tender and all the liquid has been absorbed.
4 Stir in the toasted almonds, season with black pepper and serve, garnished with a few whole almonds.

A touch of Indian spices adds extra flavour to this nutritious mixture of rice, mushroom and nuts. Try serving with Indian cauliflower on page 22.

SPICY LENTILS WITH RICE

SERVES 4

*1 tablespoon sunflower oil
350 g|12 oz carrots, finely diced
175 g|6 oz onions, finely diced
1 clove garlic
1 teaspoon cumin seeds
1½ teaspoons ground coriander
½ teaspoon turmeric
pinch paprika
225 g|8 oz long-grain brown rice
900 ml|1½ pints vegetable stock
150 g|5 oz red lentils
1 teaspoon garam masala
fresh coriander to garnish (optional)*

Preparation time **10 minutes**
Cooking time **40 minutes**

---

1 Heat the oil in a saucepan and cook the carrots, onion and garlic in it for 2 minutes over a low heat without browning.
2 Stir in the spices and cook for 1 minute. Now stir in the rice to coat the grains in the fat. Add the stock and the lentils. Bring to the boil, reduce heat and cook for 30 minutes until the rice is tender and the liquid is absorbed.
3 Turn off the heat and stir in the garam masala. Cover and leave to stand for 5 minutes. Serve at once, garnished with the coriander if you like.

A colourful supper dish full of protein, fibre and vitamin A from the carrots. This recipe originates from an Indian speciality known as Kichhari that has also been adapted to give us kedgeree, in which the lentils are replaced by smoked haddock.

Spicy lentils with rice

Per portion:

Calories 380

Fat 4g

Fibre 10g

Microwave note
Rice dishes reheat very well in the microwave. Either serve on a plate and reheat each for 4 minutes or reheat for 6 minutes in dish on full power.

Mushroom and almond pilaff

Per portion:

Calories 350

Fat 14g

Fibre 6g

CREAMY CARROT AND SWEDE

SERVES 4

675 g / 1½ lb swede, scrubbed and diced
350 g / 12 oz carrots, scrubbed and diced
knob of unsalted butter
a little skimmed milk
freshly ground black pepper
parsley sprig to garnish

Preparation time **10 minutes**
Cooking time **50 minutes**

1 Place the swede and carrots in a pan and just cover with cold water. Bring to the boil, then reduce the heat and simmer for 45 minutes until the vegetables are quite soft. Drain.
2 Mash with butter and just enough skimmed milk to make a smooth purée. Season with pepper, reheat gently in a pan and serve at once, garnished with a sprig of parsley.

Root vegetables are cheap and plentiful in winter months and this creamy purée transforms two favourite vegetables into something more sophisticated.

COLESLAW

SERVES 4

2 red-skinned dessert apples, cored and diced
juice of ½ lemon
1 small white cabbage, shredded
225 g / 8 oz carrots, scrubbed and grated
2 celery sticks, sliced
1 small onion, grated or finely chopped
100 g / 4 oz raisins
2 tablespoons natural yogurt
2 tablespoons mayonnaise
1 tablespoon chopped parsley to garnish

Preparation time **15 minutes**

1 Toss the apple in the lemon juice.
2 Mix all the prepared vegetables together with the apple, raisins, yogurt and mayonnaise. Place in a serving dish and garnish with parsley. Serve.

When the temperature drops we tend to neglect salads, but we should try to make room in our winter menus for raw vegetables with maximum vitamin C content. This classic coleslaw is easy to make, especially if you own a food processor.

WINTER SALAD BOWL

SERVES 4

275 g / 10 oz red cabbage, shredded
3 celery sticks, chopped
1 large or 2 small oranges
bunch of watercress
1 tablespoon chopped parsley
freshly ground black pepper

Preparation time **15 minutes**

1 Mix together the cabbage and celery.
2 Stand the orange(s) on a chopping board and cut away the peel. Cut into slices, then cut each slice into small pieces and add to the bowl, with any juice that has run on to the board.
3 Wash the watercress and trim any yellowing leaves and very coarse stalks. Add to the bowl with the chopped parsley and season lightly with pepper. Toss together thoroughly and serve.

Red cabbage makes just as good an ingredient in a salad as white cabbage. This colourful recipe combines oranges and watercress too, the vitamin C in the orange enhancing the way in which the body absorbs the iron in the watercress. No dressing is needed as the juice from the oranges freshens the whole salad.

Creamy carrot and swede

Per portion:

Calories 70

Fat 2g

Fibre 7g

Coleslaw

Per portion:

Calories 220

Fat 8g

Fibre 9g

Winter salad bowl

Per portion:

Calories 30

Fat 0g

Fibre 4g

Creamy carrot and swede; Winter salad bowl; Coleslaw

BEAN AND PASTA TOSS

SERVES 6

*50 g/2 oz red kidney beans, soaked
overnight
50 g/2 oz flageolet beans, soaked
overnight
50 g/2 oz wholewheat pasta shells
3 tablespoons safflower oil
1 tablespoon cider vinegar
2 teaspoons chopped fresh tarragon
1 tablespoon chopped fresh chives
pinch mustard powder*

*Preparation time **15 minutes plus
overnight soaking**
Cooking time **2¼ hours or 30 minutes***

Bean and pasta toss

Per portion:

Calories 130

Fat 7g

Fibre 5g

1 Drain both types of beans and place in two separate saucepans of cold water. Bring to the boil and boil for 10 minutes, before reducing the heat and simmering the kidney beans for 1¾–2 hours or until tender (alternatively cook in the pressure cooker at 15-lb pressure for 12 minutes). Cook the flageolet beans for 1½ hours (or for 10 minutes in the pressure cooker at 15 lb pressure). Drain both types of beans and reserve.
2 While the beans are cooking, cook the pasta in boiling water for 10–12 minutes until just tender, then drain.
3 Make the dressing while the beans and pasta are cooking. Mix the oil, vinegar, herbs and mustard in a screw-topped jar. Shake the ingredients together vigorously and pour immediately over the drained beans and pasta. Leave to cool before serving.

A substantial side salad or starter.

Bean and pasta toss;
Oriental salad

ORIENTAL SALAD

S E R V E S 4

225 g/8 oz mung beansprouts
225 g/8 oz carrots, scrubbed and cut
into matchsticks
1 green pepper, deseeded and cut
into thin strips
50 g/2 oz blanched almonds, halved
2 tablespoons sesame seeds, toasted
2 tablespoons unrefined sesame oil
2 teaspoons soy sauce
2 teaspoons cider vinegar

Preparation time **15 minutes**

1 Place the beansprouts in a bowl. Add the carrot and pepper. Mix in the almonds and sesame seeds.
2 In a screw-topped jar shake together the sesame oil, soy sauce and cider vinegar and pour over the beansprout mixture. Toss together thoroughly and serve.

A crunchy colourful salad, ideal as an accompaniment to some of the warming quiche or pastry dishes in this section.

Oriental salad	
Per portion:	
Calories 170	
Fat 13g	
Fibre 4g	

Christmas pud

Per portion:	
Calories 520	
Fat 15g	
Fibre 15g	

Apple and orange charlotte

Microwave note
Reheating Christmas pudding on Christmas Day can be done quickly in the microwave. Reheat for 4 minutes and leave to stand for 5 minutes before serving.

Fruit compote

Per portion:	
Calories 140	
Fat 0g	
Fibre 5g (approx)	

CHRISTMAS PUD

SERVES 4

175g/6oz raisins
175g/6oz sultanas
50g/2oz dried apricots, chopped
1 banana, mashed
75g/3oz Brazil nuts, chopped
100g/4oz carrots, scrubbed and finely grated
grated rind and juice of $\frac{1}{2}$ lemon
100g/4oz wholemeal breadcrumbs
25g/1oz plain wholemeal flour
2 teaspoons mixed spice
2 free-range eggs
150ml/$\frac{1}{4}$ pint skimmed milk
1 tablespoon brandy, rum or orange juice

*Preparation time **20 minutes***
*Cooking time **6 hours, plus 2 hours reheating***

1 Lightly grease a 1-kg/2-lb pudding basin. Have ready a double thickness layer of greaseproof paper to cover the top of the pudding and a pudding cloth, piece of foil or fitted lid to cover the basin.
2 Place the prepared fruit, nuts, carrot and lemon rind and juice in a large mixing bowl. Stir in the breadcrumbs, flour and spice thoroughly. Beat together the eggs, milk and brandy, rum or orange juice and pour into the bowl, mixing in well.
3 Place the mixture in a prepared basin and cover with greaseproof paper and either foil, cloth or lid. Steam for 6 hours, or cook in a pressure cooker by steaming for 30 minutes, then adding 6.75-kg/15-lb weights and cooking for a further 2 hours 45 minutes. Allow pressure to return to normal, slowly.
4 To reheat the pudding on Christmas Day, steam for 2 hours, or pressure cook at 6.75-kg/15-lb pressure for 30 minutes.
5 Serve with yogurt and decorate as shown.

Makes one 1-kg/2-lb pudding. There is no need for the conventional sugar and suet in this tasty, fruity pudding recipe.

FRUIT COMPOTE

SERVES 4

225g/8oz mixed dried fruit (prunes, apricots, pears, apple rings, figs)
600ml/1 pint cold water
juice of $\frac{1}{2}$ lemon
juice of 1 orange
pinch of mixed spice

*Preparation time **5 minutes, plus overnight standing***

1 Place the dried fruit in a bowl. Heat the water with the lemon and orange juice and the spice. Pour over the fruit and leave to stand overnight. Reheat if liked.

Dried fruits such as prunes, apricots and pears make a warming winter dessert which helps to supply fibre as well as valuable minerals. It is low in calories too.

Microwave note

Place the dried fruit in a casserole. Pour over the water, lemon and orange juice and spice. Heat on full power for 8 minutes. Leave to stand for at least 1 hour before serving.

Christmas pud; Fruit compote

APPLE AND ORANGE CHARLOTTE

SERVES 4

65 g / 2½ oz soft vegetable margarine
50 g / 2 oz desiccated coconut
100 g / 4 oz wholemeal breadcrumbs
½ teaspoon ground cinnamon
25 g / 1 oz demerara sugar
450 g / 1 lb cooking apples
1 teaspoon lemon juice
1 large orange
1 tablespoon clear honey
1 tablespoon orange juice

*Preparation time **25 minutes***
*Cooking time **30 minutes***
*Oven temperature **190 C, 375 F, gas 5***

1 Melt the margarine over a low heat and stir in the coconut, breadcrumbs and cinnamon. Stirring constantly, heat through for 5 minutes until brown and crisp. Remove from the heat and stir in the sugar.

2 Peel and finely slice the cooking apples; cover the slices in cold water mixed with the lemon juice to prevent browning. Cut away the peel from the orange and slice horizontally, then cut each slice into four quarters. Drain the apple slices and arrange in an ovenproof soufflé dish with the chopped orange. Pour over the honey and orange juice and spread the coconut mixture on top. Bake for 20–25 minutes until the apple slices are just tender. Serve at once.

A light, fruity dessert, best served hot with natural yogurt.

Microwave note

Melt the margarine in the microwave and stir in the coconut, breadcrumbs and cinnamon. Cook on full power for 2 minutes. Stir well and cook for further 1 minute. Proceed as recipe.

Apple and orange charlotte

Per portion:
Calories 360
Fat 21g
Fibre 8g

Apple and mincemeat slice

Whole recipe:

Calories 1,750	
Fat 90g	
Fibre 27g	

APPLE AND MINCEMEAT SLICE

SERVES 4

Pastry
175 g/6 oz plain wholemeal flour
75 g/3 oz soft vegetable margarine
egg yolk to bind
cold water to mix
Filling
6 tablespoons mincemeat
175 g/6 oz cooking apples, cored and grated
egg white to glaze

Preparation time **25 minutes plus 15 minutes to chill**
Cooking time **25 minutes**
Oven temperature **200 C, 400 F, gas 6**

1 Place the flour in a bowl and rub in the margarine until the mixture resembles fine breadcrumbs. Chill for 10–15 minutes. Bind with the egg yolk and a little cold water to make a soft dough.
2 Roll out two-thirds of the pastry to a 25 × 20-cm/10 × 8-in rectangle. Place in a greased Swiss roll tin, and trim the edges.
3 Put the mincemeat in a small bowl, add the apple and mix together well.
4 Spread the mincemeat mixture on the pastry, leaving 1 cm/$\frac{1}{2}$ in free all round the edge. Roll out remaining one third of the pastry and cut into strips just under 1 cm/$\frac{1}{2}$ in wide and long enough to reach diagonally across the pastry rectangle.
5 Arrange pastry strips diagonally across the mincemeat, leaving equal gaps between each strip. Flute the edges all round and glaze with the egg white.
6 Bake in the centre of the oven for 25 minutes until golden brown. Serve hot or cold.

Serve this filling slice with some natural yogurt.

ALMOND MINCE PIES

MAKES 12

Pastry
175 g/6 oz plain wholemeal flour
75 g/3 oz soft vegetable margarine
50 g/2 oz ground almonds
egg yolk to bind
cold water to mix
Filling
450 g/1 lb mincemeat
egg white to glaze
chopped blanched almonds to
decorate (optional)

Preparation time **30 minutes**
Cooking time **20–25 minutes**
Oven temperature **190 C, 375 F, gas 5**

1 Place the flour in a bowl and rub in the margarine until the mixture resembles fine breadcrumbs. Stir in the ground almonds and chill for 10–15 minutes. Bind with the egg yolk and a little cold water to make a soft dough.
2 Roll out the pastry thinly and cut out 12 circles to line patty tins. Cut out an equal number of circles to use as lids. Heat the oven to 190C, 375F, gas 5.
3 Put a small spoonful of mincemeat in each of the pastry-lined patty tins. Dampen the edges of the pastry lids and press them on top. Prick the top of the mince pies with a fork and brush with a little egg white. Sprinkle with chopped blanched almonds if you like.
4 Bake for 20–25 minutes or until the pastry is cooked and lightly browned. Remove from the tins and cool on a wire rack.

These mince pies taste best served warm. Flavour some thick-set natural yogurt with a little honey and grated orange rind to make an unusual, luscious accompaniment.

Almond mince pies	
Per mince pie:	
Calories 211	
Fat 10g	
Fibre 3g	

Apple and mincemeat slice; Almond mince pies

Christmas cake

Whole recipe:

Calories 5,300

Fat 245g

Fibre 105g

Carob yule log

Per portion:

Calories 170

Fat 6g

Fibre 1g

CHRISTMAS CAKE

MAKES 12–18 SLICES

275 g/10 oz currants
200 g/7 oz sultanas
150 g/5 oz raisins
75 g/3 oz dried pears, finely chopped
75 g/3 oz dried apricots, finely chopped
75 g/3 oz blanched almonds, finely chopped
grated rind of 1 lemon
2 tablespoons dry sherry or orange juice
200 g/7 oz plain wholemeal flour
50 g/2 oz ground almonds
1 teaspoon mixed spice
½ teaspoon ground cinnamon
¼ teaspoon grated nutmeg
175 g/6 oz soft vegetable margarine
100 g/4 oz molasses sugar
1 tablespoon clear honey
1 tablespoon molasses
4 medium free-range eggs
skimmed milk to mix

*Preparation time **40 minutes plus 8 hours or overnight soaking***
*Cooking time **2–2½ hours***
*Oven temperature **140 C, 275 F, gas 1***

1 Place the dried fruit in a bowl with the chopped almonds and lemon rind and sherry or orange juice and leave to stand for 8 hours or overnight, to let the fruit plump up and absorb the flavour of the sherry or juice.
2 Sift the flour with the ground almonds, mixed spice, cinnamon and nutmeg, adding the bran remaining in the sieve.
3 Place the margarine in a large mixing bowl with the sugar, honey and molasses and cream together until soft and fluffy. Beat in the eggs, one at a time, adding one tablespoon of the flour mixture after the first egg, and with the following three eggs.
4 Using a metal spoon, fold in the flour and prepared fruit, adding a little skimmed milk if the mixture appears a little dry. The mixture should fall off a spoon quite readily when lifted. Spoon into a greased and lined 20-cm/8-in round cake tin or an 18-cm/7-in square tin. Tie a double round of grease-proof paper around the outside of the tin to protect the cake during cooking. Press down firmly into the corners of the tin and smooth the top.
5 Bake in the oven for 2–2½ hours. Then test at 30 minute intervals with a skewer to see if the cake is cooked. If it emerges clean, the cake is ready.

A deliciously rich and moist cake, full of dried fruits and nuts. Decorate with nuts, glaze with apricot jam or clear honey and water and finish off with a bright red ribbon. The cake will store well.

CAROB YULE LOG

SERVES 7

3 free-range eggs
3 tablespoons clear honey
65 g/2½ oz plain wholemeal flour
15 g/½ oz carob powder
Filling
1 tablespoon carob powder
100 g/4 oz low-fat soft cheese
Topping
2 (60-g/2½-oz) carob and orange bars
175 g/6 oz low-fat soft cheese

*Preparation time **40 minutes***
*Cooking time **8–10 minutes***
*Oven temperature **220 C, 425 F, gas 7***

1 Place the eggs and honey in a large mixing bowl and whisk together. If beating by hand the mixture will whip quicker if placed over a pan of hot water; if you are using an electric mixer, there is no need to do this. Continue whisking until the mixture is thick, pale and smooth. Test by trailing the mixture into a letter 'W'; if when you make the last stroke, the first stroke is still visible, then the mixture is ready.
2 Sift the flour and carob powder together and using a metal spoon gently fold into the mixture.
3 When thoroughly blended in, pour the mixture into a greased and lined Swiss roll tin and bake for 8–10 minutes.
4 Test the sponge after 8 minutes. It should be golden brown and spring back when touched. If it is ready, invert the tin over a piece of greaseproof paper.

Remove tin and lining paper and trim away 5 mm/¼ in all round. Make a slit 2.5 cm/l in from the bottom of the sponge and place the second sheet of paper on top. Roll up gently, but firmly, and leave wrapped in the paper until cold.

5 Now make the filling. Beat the carob powder in the soft cheese. Carefully unwrap the roll, spread the soft cheese mixture inside and roll up again.

6 Make the topping. Place two-thirds of the carob and orange bars in a bowl over a pan of hot water and melt. Beat in the soft cheese and spread on top of the roll. Mark with a fork. Grate the remaining carob and sprinkle on top. Leave to set, before serving sliced. Eat the same day.

A healthy, caffeine-free, wholemeal version of a traditional Christmas favourite.

Christmas cake; Carob yule log

Shortbread

Per piece:

Calories 78

Fat 5g

Fibre 1g

SHORTBREAD

MAKES 12 PIECES

90 g / 3½ oz plain wholemeal flour
15 g / ½ oz rice flour (brown)
75 g / 3 oz unsalted butter or vegetable margarine
2 teaspoons muscovado sugar

*Preparation time **20 minutes***
*Cooking time **20–25 minutes***
*Oven temperature **180 C, 350 F, gas 4***

1 Sift the flours together into a bowl, adding the bran remaining in the sieve. Rub in the butter or margarine until the mixture resembles fine breadcrumbs.
2 Stir in the sugar. Using your hands, bring the mixture together to form a smooth dough and then knead lightly.
3 Pat the dough out to fit a lightly greased 18-cm/7-in shallow square tin and smooth the top. Prick with a fork and cut into 12 fingers (alternatively place the mixture in a round sandwich tin and mark into 10 segments).
4 Bake in the centre of the oven for 20–25 minutes. Retrace the markings and leave to cool in the tin. Remove and store the shortbread in an airtight tin. It will keep fresh for up to 10 days.

A light crumbly shortbread which is full of fibre.

Shortbread; Christmas flapjack

CHRISTMAS FLAPJACK

MAKES 8

75 g / 3 oz soft vegetable margarine
3 tablespoons mincemeat
1 tablespoon clear honey
175 g / 6 oz rolled oats

Preparation time **5 minutes**
Cooking time **30 minutes**
Oven temperature **160 C, 325 F, gas 3**

1 Melt the margarine with the mincemeat and honey. Stir in the oats and then remove from the heat.
2 Spread the mixture into a lightly greased 20-cm/8-in square cake tin or an 18-cm/7-in round tin and bake for 20–25 minutes until golden brown.
3 Cool in the tin on a wire rack and mark the flapjack into 8 fingers. Store in an airtight container for up to 10 days.

An unusual, moreish addition to the Christmas tea table.

Christmas flapjack

Per portion:

Calories 190

Fat 10g

Fibre 2g

Cheese biscuits;
Hazelnut rolls

HAZELNUT ROLLS

MAKES 12

Pastry
100 g/4 oz plain wholemeal flour
50 g/2 oz soft vegetable margarine
cold water to mix
Filling
1 teaspoon sunflower oil
50 g/2 oz onion, finely chopped
50 g/2 oz button mushrooms, finely chopped
50 g/2 oz carrots, grated
50 g/2 oz ground hazelnuts
50 g/2 oz wholemeal breadcrumbs
1 tablespoon chopped parsley
½ teaspoon dried thyme
freshly ground black pepper
1 free-range egg
sesame seeds to garnish (optional)

Preparation time **30 minutes plus 15 minutes to chill**
Cooking time **20–25 minutes**
Oven temperature **200 C, 400 F, gas 6**

1 Sift the flour into a mixing bowl and add the bran remaining in the sieve. Rub the margarine into the flour, until the mixture resembles fine breadcrumbs. Chill for 10–15 minutes.
2 Heat the oil in a saucepan and cook the onion over a low heat for 2 minutes, without browning. Stir in the chopped mushrooms and continue to cook until the juices run from the mushrooms. Transfer to a bowl and add the grated carrot, ground hazelnuts, breadcrumbs, parsley and thyme. Mix in thoroughly and season with pepper.
3 Beat the egg and add half to the bowl, reserving the remainder as a glaze. Bind the mixture together, divide it into two and using a little wholemeal flour to prevent it from sticking, roll each half to a sausage shape, 20-cm/8-in long.
4 Take the pastry mixture out of the refrigerator. Add about four teaspoons cold water and stir in with a knife. Bring the mixture together, adding extra water to make a soft dough.
5 Transfer to a lightly floured surface and roll out to a 20 × 15-cm/8 × 6-in rectangle. Cut in half lengthwise and place the two rolls of filling on each.

Brush the pastry with cold water and lift one side to seal with the other edge. Knock back the edges with a knife, flute and cut each into 6 pieces.
6 Place on a greased baking tray and snip steam holes in the top. Brush with the remaining beaten egg and, if liked, scatter a few sesame seeds on top.
7 Bake in the oven for about 15–20 minutes, until the pastry is golden.

A vegetarian alternative to the always popular sausage roll.

CHEESE BISCUITS

MAKES ABOUT 26 SMALL BISCUITS

100 g/4 oz plain wholemeal flour
40 g/1½ oz soft vegetable margarine
40 g/1½ oz Double Gloucester or Red Leicester cheese, grated
pinch of cayenne
pinch mustard powder
1 free-range egg yolk
skimmed milk to mix and glaze
sesame seeds and poppy seeds to garnish

Preparation time **20 minutes**
Cooking time **8–10 minutes**
Oven temperature **200 C, 425 F, gas 7**

1 Place the flour in a bowl and rub in the margarine, until the mixture resembles fine breadcrumbs. Stir in the grated cheese, cayenne and mustard. Add the egg yolk and bind the mixture to a fairly moist dough, using your hands to draw the mixture together. If the mixture seems a little dry, add a dash of skimmed milk.
2 Roll out on a lightly floured surface to 3 mm/⅛ in thick and stamp out shapes using a small square or round cutter. Transfer to 2 greased baking trays.
3 Glaze the biscuits with skimmed milk and garnish with some sesame or poppy seeds.
4 Bake in the centre of the oven for 8–10 minutes until golden brown. Cool on a wire rack. The biscuits will stay fresh if kept in an airtight container for 10 days.

Hazelnut rolls
Per roll:
Calories 95
Fat 6g
Fibre 2g

Freezing note
Freeze down the uncooked biscuits ready-cut and then bake straight from frozen when needed.

Cheese biscuits
Whole recipe:
Calories 790
Fat 53g
Fibre 10g

Nutritional Value of Vegetable Protein Foods

The chart below compares 100 g/4 oz of various foods for fat, fibre, protein and calorie content.

In addition to the reduced fat content of certain vegetarian protein foods, the fibre content is significantly higher.

Relating these contents back to the advice given on pages 6 and 7, it can be seen that a diet based on vegetarian proteins offers a healthy alternative to a meat-based diet.

ANIMAL VERSUS VEGETABLE FOODS per 100 g/4 oz

	Fat (%)	Fibre(%)	Protein (%)	Calories
Beef	24	0	16	280
Chicken	4	0	20	120
Cod	0.7	0	17	76
Herring	17	0	17	234
Milk (whole)	3.8	0	3.3	65
Cheddar cheese	33	0	26	406
Eggs	10	0	12	147
Wholemeal flour	2	9.6	13	318
Brown rice	1.9	0.9	7.5	360
Haricot beans (raw weight)	1.6	25	21	271
Lentils (raw weight)	1	11.7	23	304
Walnuts (shelled weight)	50	5	10	525